PUT MORE CASH IN YOUR POCKET

...RE CASH
IN YOUR
POCKET

Turn What You Know into Dough

LORAL LANGEMEIER

HARPER

BUSINESS

NEW YORK • LONDON • TORONTO • SYDNEY

HARPER

BUSINESS

PUT MORE CASH IN YOUR POCKET. Copyright © 2009 by Loral Langemeier. Foreword copyright © 2009 by Harry S. Dent. All rights reserved. Printed in the United States of America. No part of this book may be used or reproduced in any manner whatsoever without written permission except in the case of brief quotations embodied in critical articles and reviews. For information address HarperCollins Publishers, 10 East 53rd Street, New York, NY 10022.

HarperCollins books may be purchased for educational, business, or sales promotional use. For information please write: Special Markets Department, HarperCollins Publishers, 10 East 53rd Street, New York, NY 10022.

FIRST EDITION

Designed by Level C

Library of Congress Cataloging-in-Publication Data has been applied for.

ISBN 978-0-06-176325-0

14 15 16 17 18   OV/RRD   10 9 8 7 6 5 4

To all those people out there who
want to make their lives a little bit easier.

And to my husband, Carl, and our fabulous children,
Logan and Tristin, who support and encourage me always.
Thank you.

ACKNOWLEDGMENTS

The best part of my journey has been the people I've had the good fortune to meet and know. I love going to work every day and spending time with talented and enthusiastic entrepreneurs and teammates. As anyone who's written a book knows, it takes a lot of time, but with the right team, it's a bit easier. I want to thank everyone who helped me get this book to the shelf. I'd be remiss to think I can thank everyone who helped here, but since I get a page to try, I'll mention a few.

A huge thanks to everyone at HarperCollins, especially Hollis Heimbouch and Matthew Inman. Thanks to Caroline Sherman for putting the pieces together, again. Thank you also to Jay Mandel and the team at William Morris. And to Lisa Sanderson and Jamie Mandelbaum. Thanks to Mark Levine for your collaboration and assistance on the book.

I am so very grateful for the wonderful world of Live Out Loud, the members of which continue to support me and one another with dedication, commitment, energy, and innovation. Thank you to every member of our Live Out Loud community, including members of Loral's Big Table and the numerous Cash Machine teams. Thanks to the entire Live Out Loud staff, Premier Mentoring, and all the coaches and Field Partners, including Will Mattox, Sue Walker, Janet Fish, Fred Auzenne, Rebekah Hall, Wendy Byford, Gary Bauer, Jim Griffin and 54Freedom team, Kirby Cochran and the Castle Arch team, Robert Couch, Martha Hanlon, Steve Parker, Paul Miltonberger, David Babinski, James Sheppard, Mark Nichols, and Chris Williams. All of you contribute so much with your enthusiasm and expertise.

Thank you to my mom; my sister, Holly; and my brothers, Jeff, Doug, and Kent; and a big hug and thanks to my dad, whom I miss so much. Special thanks to my Aunt Bev, for pushing me to push myself.

Of course, the most lovely part of the journey is at home, and I'm forever grateful for my husband, Carl, and our children, Logan and Tristin. Thank you for being there for me, and with me, always.

CONTENTS

FOREWORD

As a leading-edge economist, I work with numbers. I can tell you of the complex cycles that our economy has faced over time and what is critical in each time period. I've spent my career studying the numbers and sharing my findings. There's a logic to our economy that includes inflation and deflation, bubbles and depressions, and periods of growth and times of recession.

But what do you do with this type of macro information? You can have all the facts and figures in the world, but if you don't have a tactical plan to prosper, you won't.

Facts and figures give you knowledge and a sense of the landscape ahead; Loral gives you a plan to engage that knowledge. She turns facts and figures from numbers on a page into information that you can put to use for your advantage. Her advice is clear, concise, and actionable, which is what is needed to put more money in your pocket, thrive in economic upturns, survive economic downturns, and create wealth in the long term.

If you're like most, recent economic events have shaken you up a bit. You realize that traditional means of making money may no longer apply. We've seen the economy boom and crash, not once but many times. The dips and turns are to be expected. History repeats itself and the next decade will be more like the 1930s, when major companies and banks failed *but* entrepreneurialism flourished—and more at the everyday scale than massive new Microsoft and Google companies.

Traditional methods to achieve financial security, now and in the future, can no longer to be relied upon as they once were. Job security seems a thing of the past. Baby boomers believed that their homes and other investments would contribute most, if not all, of their retirement funds. Today they face the possibility that retirement is out of reach for a while.

What Loral recommends makes sense. You need to learn how to put more money in your pocket as quickly as possible. She recommends that you don't spend time learning a new trade but put the knowledge and skills that you have right now into an entrepreneurial endeavor. Start now, don't wait—whether you believe the economy is getting healthier or not. Find a marketable skill among those that you possess, run with it, and be more creative in how you apply and market that skill.

Along with having quantifiable strategies, Loral has a knack for helping people find the right Cash Machine to suit their particular skills. She has an eye for spotting trends, which helps immensely in positioning. She has the ability to take you out of your comfort zone because she will also help you see the possibilities ahead and the capability within you.

Put More Cash in Your Pocket is a guide to your future if you act on it. No longer do we have the luxury to sit back and wait for things to get better. What you need to do is get moving—get doing. I see the future as one where you need to be able to count on yourself. And even though many have found themselves in too much debt as the economy has slowed, increasing your cash flow and income is far more important in a new era wherein cash, cash flow, and credit will be the key to both survival and taking advantage of the greatest sale in history on financial assets and new business trends.

Loral will help you awaken your resilience, uncover your strengths, summon up your courage, engage your imagination, and bring to fruition your entrepreneurial goals.

I advise you to take action starting now. Read this book from cover to cover. You'll know where to go from there.

Harry S. Dent Jr., president of the H. S. Dent Foundation and bestselling author of *The Great Boom Ahead*, *The Roaring 2000s*, *The Great Depression Ahead*, and *The Next Great Bubble Boom*

INTRODUCTION

If you could find a way to put $500 to $1,000 in your pocket right now, this month, would you do it? How about $500 to $1,000 in your pocket every single month for an entire year? And then next year? And the year after that? Maybe even increasing that amount month after month?

Yes, yes, yes, yes, and yes. Right? I mean, of course. Who wouldn't want that extra cash?

I'm here to tell you that it is not only possible to do exactly that, but that it will definitely happen if you follow the steps in this book. This is not a boast or a brag. I've helped thousands of people make extra cash fast. People from all different backgrounds, in a variety of situations, all over the world. People just like you.

And I'll do it by helping you to make your life bigger, not smaller. In fact, with the process I'm going to share with you:

- You do not have to scrimp and save.

- You do not have to borrow from one part of your life to pay for another.

- You do not have to worry over decisions you made in the past.

- You get to see yourself create new cash.

- You discover a new, and fun, way to spend time with your family and friends.

- You get a new lease on life.

This isn't about putting money under your mattress, sewing your own clothes, or sacrificing that latte you love so much. Nope. This is about taking the skills and knowledge you already have, and turning those into cash—today.

Whether you are a single parent juggling work and home, a young adult eager to get a foothold in life, or a senior living on a fixed income, this book can change your life. If you do work that supports you, but the money you make isn't quite enough to help you send your kids to college, or make the home improvements you need, or even pay for a nice vacation, this book is for you. If you are older and your dreams have crashed with the stock market, or you are younger and constantly playing catch-up with your money, this book will change your life for the oh-so-much better.

My proven process for making money fast can, at the very least, set you on the road to financial certainty. At best, it can help you create wealth. And by *you* I mean anyone with desire, energy, and a positive mind-set.

In order to make $500 to $1,000 extra a month, you don't need to understand finance. You don't need to understand economics. You just need to manage your time and energy into a money-making venture based 100 percent on the skills and knowledge you *already* have. And you can do this while you're working, while you're parenting, and while you're trying to fit in that thirty minutes of exercise, gardening, or quiet time every day.

I believe you can do this because I did it. And it dramatically changed my life.

I wasn't born with money, I didn't grow up around wealth, and I'm certainly not an Ivy League–educated money manager or big-city financial professional. I'm a Nebraska farm girl who woke up early every morning to do chores before school because, as my grandfather reminded us, "You don't eat until the animals eat." And I liked breakfast.

In high school I also worked outside the farm to support myself. I felt lucky to have an entrepreneurial spirit and I was able to create a lawn-mowing business that made some good money. Okay, so maybe its success was based on the fact that I created a niche by targeting lawns no one else wanted to mow . . . cemeteries. But still. Then in college, I created a business out of my interest in fitness. And when I graduated, I had a wellness business that did quite, um, well.

But the truth was I spent most of my young adult life just making it. In fact, as recently as 1995, I had little to my name except my car, a few small pieces of what I called furniture, and my clothes. Four years later, I was a single mom. It was then that I turned my life around and committed to do better than just get by. And today, I create the money to live the life of my dreams.

Along the way, though, I realized that some people don't want to create wealth. They just want to make a bit more money every month. And they want to make that money fast. Fortunately for me, as I worked out my system for making a lot of money, I also made a wonderful discovery—a surefire way for anyone and everyone to make $500 to $1,000 extra cash every single month for the rest of their lives. And that process is what this book is about.

I came to this insight through a lot of trial and error. But fortunately, I never let mistakes get in my way. I learned from them and moved on. That tenacity came from the farm, where I learned how to work hard, I learned about teamwork, and I learned to be resourceful. But I also had to overcome a lot of bad thinking.

In my family, we hardly ever talked about money. And when we did, the phrase "we can't afford it" was the dominant theme. This was frustrating for me. I later learned that I could afford anything I wanted, if I just made more money to pay for it. Now all of the people I've coached and trained to make more money never say "I can't afford it." Because they can. This phrase is no longer a part of their vocabulary. It should no longer be a part of yours. The idea that you need to tighten your belt is the exact opposite of what you will believe after you read this book. As I said in *The Secret*, money comes easily and frequently it will. You will know that you can have what you want, and you will know how to get it.

When I was younger, I was always curious about money: where it came from, how it was made, who made it, how it was managed, and how a little bit of money could become a lot of money. Since money talk was nonexistent in my house, as it is in most of the homes in this country, I learned a lot of this by finding the answers from people outside my family. These included local business leaders in my hometown (I even went to work at the local bank) and then, when I was older, top leaders in the financial industry. When there was a person I admired and wanted to get to know, I'd go out of my way to meet him or her. I'd arrange meetings at their offices, even if only for fifteen minutes. I'd prepare specific questions the night before so I wouldn't waste my time or theirs. And little by little I started to figure some things out. I went to college on a basketball scholarship and studied business administration and finance. I also taught aerobics and worked as a personal trainer on the side. And decided to get a masters degree in exercise physiology.

When I finished school, I contacted the Cooper Institute in Dallas, the nation's preeminent aerobic exercise research organization, and asked for an internship. They turned me down. I persisted, telling them I'd work for free until I proved myself. They accepted, and I packed up my car and drove down to Texas. Soon they were paying me. With that experience under my belt, I went back to the bank for which I had worked in my late teens and early twenties, and asked them to contract with me to set up a health and fitness program for their employees. They agreed. I approached a number of other companies and organizations and did the same, creating my first successful full-time venture.

One day I got a telephone call from an oil and gas company, asking me if I was interested in bidding on a contract to establish nutrition and fitness programs for its offshore oil rigs. I'd never heard of the company; we didn't have their gas stations in Nebraska. I later discovered that they were, in fact, legitimate. More than legitimate: They were a Fortune 500 energy company. I'd never been to New Orleans, and I was intrigued.

When I got off the airplane several executives met me on the tarmac. They led me to a van, handed me steel-tipped shoes and a hard hat, and drove me to a helicopter. We then flew offshore. I don't know if you've ever seen the offshore world of oil rigs, but it's like a little city out there. One of the first things I noticed were these huge vats.

I pushed the button on my headset microphone. "What's in those?"

"Lard," one of the executives said. "We cook with that."

I saw immediately why they needed me. We landed on a few of the rigs, I talked to several of the employees, and then we flew back to shore. The man who'd called me didn't waste any time explaining the situation. "Look," he said. "We have all these rigs, and men, and we need nutrition and a fitness centers on all these rigs."

That was progressive, I thought.

He went on. "It costs us $60,000 for every back injury," he said. "We need to do this and we want you."

I was shocked. I was twenty-four years old and had less than no clue. I couldn't even read the contract they gave me, except for the paragraph that said the budget for the project went well into seven figures. A little voice inside me whispered: *Just say yes and figure it out later.*

I share this story because I think that people often under-value the power of a personal approach. And if nothing else, you have the power to be personal. When you read this book and learn the way to make more money fast, you'll see the appeal of being personal, of being assertive and persistent, and of creating a team with others who can and—though they might not know it yet—will want to help you.

Unfortunately, I was too successful with this oil and gas com-pany, which led them to offer me a full-time job, which led me to say yes, which led me to feel the quick enclosure of four walls and fluorescent lighting. Well, not *too* quick: I stayed there five years. And I'm glad for it. I learned a lot about business: opera-tions, management, finance, sales, and marketing. It was a good education and they paid me. But it was not the life I wanted.

After attending some financial and leadership seminars, I de-cided to study career and financial coaching and soon became a Certified Master Coach. While still holding my day job at the oil and gas company, I was coaching before work, at lunchtime, and after work. And I hadn't stopped my personal training venture, that family mantra about working hard still echoing in my head.

Eventually, I created my own seminar business. I traveled the globe telling people that the attitudes toward money they'd in-herited and been taught may be holding them back. Money isn't scarce, it's abundant. Money isn't the root of all evil, it's the seed of a lot of good. And making it can even be fun. Money isn't just something other people know about, it's something everyone can learn about. Money can improve life. Money can solve problems. And most of all, money should not be taboo. Money is a conversation that needs to be had, out loud. I even named my company Live Out Loud. And with that company and the community we created, I helped people generate wealth for themselves and their families.

But then a couple of years ago, I noticed something different was happening at my seminars. My traditional workshops and events were focused on creating great wealth, generating millions even. But new people started showing up at the seminars and logging onto my online forums. People probably a lot like you. These people were struggling just to pay the bills. And though they thought millions might be nice one day, right now they just wanted to make a little more cash. They were people who realized they didn't have enough money to stop working and didn't see how they ever would. They were living paycheck to paycheck. And sometimes, credit card to paycheck, or worse. It became obvious to me that these people had a lot of potential. But they weren't using it.

I knew I had to do something. And that's when I decided to write this book. A simple, straightforward plan to make $500 to $1,000 extra cash a month.

How?

It's easier than you think.

You have everything you need.

ONE

————

MAKE MORE MONEY

You don't have fixed potential, why accept a fixed income? You can bring more money into your life. It's not difficult. Especially when you follow a specific approach, the one presented in this book, to generate an extra $500 to $1,000 a month.

There is opportunity everywhere. In difficult times, that may not be easy to see. But it's true. In fact, difficult times can create even more opportunity. And when you discover your potential to make more money and identify the opportunities that can collide with your abilities, you can create cash, fast.

Some days are not easy days. As I'm writing this book, the economy is floundering, banks are failing, and people are worried. But whether the economy is up or down in any given month, the fact that you picked up this book makes me think your personal financial situation is not where you want it to be. Chances are, you are feeling pressure on your finances. This can be frustrating and for many, a little scary. But what's even scarier is when I hear too many people having the wrong conversation. What I'm hearing is "Should I save or should I spend?" By cornering yourself in that conversation, between those two choices, you limit all of your choices. That's the wrong question. The right question is this "How do I make more money?" When you have an attitude of growth, rather than shrinking, everything opens up to you.

I'm not one to dangle false hope. I assure you, there has never been a better time for you to make more money, fast. There is great reason for hope, even if you can't see it just yet. By the end of this book, you will. And you'll also come to realize that with a little more money—$500, $1,000 a month—you will start to feel more optimistic.

THE KEY TO MAKING MORE MONEY IS TO DO WHAT YOU ALREADY KNOW HOW TO DO, WITH A TWIST.

The twist is that you are going to get paid to do those things. And so if you have a skill you use at work that you can use in additional ways you've not thought of, or a skill you have that you use outside of work, or a hobby you enjoy, or even a chore that you seem to undertake well, you are going to use that to create cash fast. It's this technique, not saving or scrimping, that's going to help you make more money and get on track toward the life you want.

The steps work like this:

a. Uncover the skill(s) you have.

b. Come up with a money-making idea around your skill(s).

c. Test if that idea can make money fast.

d. Execute that idea immediately.

e. Perfect the idea later.

Scrimping and saving is not the only answer.

When finances get tight, the easiest—and most reflexive—thing to do is to scrimp and save. This is the *opposite* of what you need to do to breathe easier. The best thing you can do when finances get tight is to focus on making more money.

Basically, there are two parts to money in your life: the money that flows in (your income) and the money that flows out (your expenses).

In my experience, most people focus too much on the money that flows out when they should put their time and energy into the money that flows in. For example, let's say you want a new dishwasher. You need a new dishwasher. And I don't mean replacing your spouse. I mean the machine. When in need of a new dishwasher, many people will choose to cut back on another expense so they can afford the dishwasher. They'll wait to fix the car, or give up the paint job on the house.

There is no need to do that. There is no need to decrease your outflow of money. That is a negative use of time, energy, and ability. It is better to be positive and focus on how to increase the inflow of money to you. An extra $500 to $1,000 a month is out there, waiting for you. Let's get it to flow into your pockets, because $500 to $1,000 extra a month could go a long way toward getting a new dishwasher, fixing the car, *and* painting the house.

There is nothing sadder, to me, than watching hopeful human beings take advice to cut off their dreams and redirect their spirit to getting small.

I AM HERE TO TELL YOU THAT YOU ABSOLUTELY, POSITIVELY CAN STAY IN YOUR DREAMS AND GET BIGGER.

I don't know about you, but I don't think it's a lot of fun to restrict my life. Not that I live extravagantly, but I do like the simple pleasures: a latte, a weekend movie, new shoes now and then. These things shouldn't give me stress. And they don't. Because when I need or want something, I generate more cash to pay for it. I don't save for it or pay for it with a credit card. I go and make the money. And it's always easier than I think it's going to be.

Dealing with Debt

There is so much judgment around credit card debt these days. I actually find it motivating. When I see clients with credit card debt I know they want a big life; they just don't know how to pay for it yet. Instead of suggesting to clients that they give up their lives and focus solely on paying off that debt, I suggest they go make more money to pay off that debt.

When you realize you can make money fast, an extra $500 to $1,000 of new money every month, you will also realize you can use a lot of that new money to pay down credit card debt.

High-interest debt is the most toxic hurdle to financial recovery. Most people have financial pressure that goes beyond a desire to get a dishwasher. Many are dealing with paying back money they borrowed for their education, loans from a big purchase like a car or entertainment center, or even money they owe for healthcare. Debt is draining. It creates stress both physically and mentally, and it can be very distracting. I advise everyone to deal with debt in the exact same way—get rid of high-interest debt such as credit card debt, and manage well the low-interest debt such as mortgages or home equity loans.

Easier said than done? If you're making $500 to $1,000 extra a month, imagine how much easier it would be to pay off those credit cards. Once you start making this cash, fast, you will be able to direct some of that money to getting rid of your credit card debt. I strongly recommend you use an easy debt-elimination plan like the one I offer for free on www.liveoutloud.com. This is an efficient and effective way to get rid of credit card debt. And because it's methodical and proven, you'll stay motivated and engaged in the process. With the $500 to $1,000 extra a month you'll be making, you'll find this debt-elimination process very doable. Soon enough you'll be debt free and better able to manage your lower interest debts like mortgage payments or school loans, and start buying things you want without scrimping and saving. The best part is you will be excited and reenergized daily because you'll be making more money, getting rid of financial problems, and acquiring the things you want to make your life easier and better.

A community of self-reliance is self-fulfilling.

In addition to promoting saving or scrimping, too many financial experts rely on the markets for making money. The markets, whether we're talking about the stock market or the real estate market or any other arena where investors are subject to emotional swings and forces beyond their control, are not reliable places to make more money. Historically, the markets have created money for some people and lost money for others. But if you want a sure thing, a way to make a definite $500 to $1,000 a month, then you need to rely on one thing you can be sure of, and that is yourself.

And contrary to popular belief, that doesn't have to be a lonely prospect. I believe strongly in creating a community of self-reliance. That is, relying on your skills and ideas while enrolling others who can support you and whom you can support in their efforts. This country was built on self-reliance, on the backs of men and women who used their skills to make things better. This is a great country because the people who built the core of it didn't play games or speculate. They knew what they wanted and they created it. This attitude is the American spirit, and you are going to grab a piece of the American spirit and make your life better.

My community calls this "living out loud": the idea that you can be in a conversation that focuses on relying on yourself and your community, and creating abundance.

And so now you know:

- You will create $500 to $1,000 of new money every month.

- You will not be saving.

- You will not be scrimping.

- You will focus on money coming to you through income.

- You will be using your skills and potential to create that new money.

Let's consider some examples. I present four case studies throughout this book. These are composites of real clients, with names changed to protect the money makers. We'll follow each of these, chapter to chapter, to help you better understand your own approach to making new money, fast.

_____

MADELINE MATHEWS
Not Quite Enough

Madeline Mathews had socked away some of her salary into stocks. Then, unfortunately, the stocks shrank to half their value before she was able to tell her broker to sell them. Divorced, mid-forties, Madeline had hoped the stocks would help her pay for her kids' education as well as add a cushion to her teacher's pension so that she could stop working in ten or fifteen years. Her schedule was a bit grueling and she wasn't sure how much longer she could keep it up. Madeline taught high school social studies in a suburb of Boston, Massachusetts. She oversaw several after-school activities, including the debating club and Students Against Drunk Driving, and was a parent to three kids, ages twelve to sixteen. An engaging teacher, Madeline was popular with the students, and their enthusiasm for her classes kept her energized.

Not one to complain, Madeline prevailed on a course of "work hard for your money." She was also grateful for the security of her job, its healthcare benefits, and its pension. Though she was not well off, Madeline's mortgage, household expenses, and—for now—the needs of her children were manageable. But she wanted more than manageable. She wanted to have extra money for the essentials that were sneaking up on her, such as her kids' education and her after-work years (I don't use the word "retirement" because I think it sounds like you're being put out to pasture). Madeline also wanted extra money for the not-essential-but-sure-would-be-nice things, including some dinners out, clothes when the kids wanted them and not just when they needed them, and a possible vacation for the family. She also wanted to make more money with the hope of creating more time for herself. Even in the summer, when she was off work, Madeline found her days full, doing house projects she'd neglected all year or carpooling her children here and there.

After losing a lot of her cushion in the stock market, Madeline decided to cut back on her spending in order to save more money. She stopped getting her monthly manicure and pedicure, went less often to her beauty salon, washed her clothes inside out to make them last longer, and stopped her gym membership, vowing to do morning yoga at home and take runs around the neighborhood. After a month of this, Madeline was still falling short financially, with the added bonus of feeling frumpy and out of shape.

I met with Madeline just about then.

Loral's Coaching Clip

"I don't know any other way," Madeline said.

I asked Madeline if she was happy this way. She shook her head. "Definitely not."

"What if I could help you make $500 to $1,000 extra a month, would that help?"

Her look verged on sarcastic and I think it was all she could do to suppress a "duh." "Of course," she said, "a lot."

"What would you do with that money?" I asked.

She shook her head. "I don't know," she said. "I'm careful not to want what I don't have. That's how I keep the credit cards under control."

"And is that fun?" I asked. "Stomping on your dreams? Even the small ones?"

"No, of course not," she said.

"Then tell me what you would do with an extra $1,000 a month."

Collecting her thoughts, Madeline took a moment. "Okay," she said. "I'd like to put $200 into an education fund for each of the three kids. Then I'd put $100 into a fund for when I finish teaching. And then I'd—wait, do I have to pay taxes on it?"

"Yes," I said. "But you're also going to have expenses against this revenue, so you might not have as much tax as you think."

"Okay. Well, I guess of the remaining $300 some would go to taxes, and then maybe I'd start allocating money toward a family vacation, and maybe put some money toward stuff the kids always seem to want, you know, like clothes, technology, sports equipment, stuff like that."

"Sounds good," I said.

"I'm a teacher and single parent, Loral, with little time to brush my hair. How am I going to make $1,000 extra a month?"

"You will," I promised.

———

One of the terrible consequences of financial frustration is that it makes some people stop dreaming. They just cut off their wants, scrimp back on their needs, and hunker down into a smaller, apparently safer life. But guess what? Small is not safe. Small is not secure. Small is just small. Scrimping and saving keeps you small. And when you live small, you limit your potential, you cut off your opportunities, and you do an incredible disservice to yourself. Cutting off your dreams is unnecessarily cruel to yourself and those who may model themselves after you.

We spend a lot of time talking about the American Dream, but unfortunately, this is sometimes undermined by the American Fear. Fear of what? Fear of, well, just who you are exactly. Perhaps you've been what I call a W-2 your whole life. You've worked a job that's become your identity. And because you identify with that job, that's where you put your focus and your attention. "I'm John who works at Gold Bank. VP, yep. Ten years." The concern then becomes this: What if you put your focus and attention on something else, like making new money? You're John who works at Gold Bank, who by the way happens to fix motorcycles at night to make new money. Do you really want to be known as the motorcycle fix-it guy? Did you go to college for that? But let me tell you this: Unless you put your focus and attention, your intention, on your objective, what you want to have and achieve, then you will not achieve that objective.

YOU MUST GIVE ATTENTION TO YOUR INTENTION.

It may be difficult to realign your identity. I've heard more than several people state what they do for a living, then whisper, "But I'm also starting this small business." It's important to live out loud about what you are trying to achieve. If you are worried about success, then let's hope big success becomes the biggest worry you ever have.

Life can change for you. You can have a better life, an easier life, less stress, more fun, more of what you need, and more of what you want. And you can do this by starting out simple, by focusing on the approach in this book to make an extra $1,000 a month.

An extra $12,000 a year is significant no matter how much you make now. And as I've said, this is money you can be making right now, by just using skills you already have. And it's not money that's been redirected away from other parts of your life. This is new money. Extra cash. Let's say you currently make $40,000. And last year, you tried the scrimping and saving plan and managed to put $5,000 of that into the bank. You may think you're $5,000 for the better, right? But are you? Was it really worth it to give up going to the movies, to not have the family vacation, to see your daughter wearing jeans with three tears in them instead of the two that are in fashion? I'm sure it wasn't.

Now's the time to choose to use your abilities, your capacity, your energy, your desire, and your time to focus on making new money and bringing a big dose of hope and optimism into your life.

Let's check in on our second case study.

———

ANNE AND DEAN LARGO
Still Seeking the American Dream

Anne and Dean Largo were frustrated. They couldn't understand why they hadn't achieved their goals. High school sweethearts who married right after school, they thought they had everything planned out. Now in their mid-thirties, with two kids, they felt no more secure than they had ten years earlier. And they were worried that they'd missed some "life course" along the way.

After working a few years in fashion retail, Anne was now a stay-at-home mom for their two girls, who were in elementary school. Dean supported the family managing one of the large grocery stores in town, a suburb south of Gary, Indiana. They rented one half of a two-family house a few blocks from the store. Dean's hours were manageable, usually no more than forty to fifty a week, but his annual salary wasn't increasing at the rate he'd expected when he was first hired right out of high school. The parent company seemed to have constant cutbacks, and Dean was always worried about keeping his job.

Dean's job was stifling, their small home was cramped, and the Largos still felt like they were just kids, playing house. They didn't feel free or secure as adults, and they had no plan for their future. Anne managed the family budget, but was in a constant cycle with the credit cards. No matter how much she paid off the debt, or stopped using the card, there always seemed to be a $3,000 balance just sitting there. They even did most of their own personal care, such as cutting the kids' hair at home, and home projects, such as mowing the lawn, themselves, in order to save money. Dean had a commercial power washer he inherited from a former neighbor that he used to keep the house, the fence, and even the driveway looking clean and new with little mainte-nance. In the two months out of the year he did this chore, not only did Dean get his childhood firefighter fantasy fed, but his landlord took $100 off the rent.

Their big dream was to get their own home in a nicer neigh-borhood, save money for the kids' school, and own a car that ran consistently.

The Largos excited me. Here were two hardworking parents who just wanted things to be a little bit easier. I knew they had the energy and the desire to make more money, and I also saw right away that they had the potential to make $1,000 in cash every month. This would give them a great step up toward their goals of having their own home and putting some money into a fund for their kids' education. The potential was right there, in black and white. And I couldn't wait to tell them about it.

————

HELEN GREEN
Growing Old Isn't for Wimps

When Helen Green's husband died, he'd left her with a mortgage-free condo in Florida, a retirement account he'd set up as a family doctor in private practice, a mutual fund, and a broken heart. Alone for the first time ever, she wondered how she'd survive. After a year, she finally felt some semblance of control again. Helen sold her husband's share of his medical practice and was able to enjoy a life without working. She had an active social life and at first felt free from economic pressures. Her husband's investments and Social Security provided enough cash flow for her to live comfortably. Helen redecorated her apartment and bought a new car. She volunteered at a local hospital and joined a bridge club.

But several years later, things changed. Income from her husband's investments dropped. Two bad hurricane seasons in a row prompted Helen's homeowner's and auto insurance carriers to pull out of the state. The only insurance she could find cost three times what she'd previously paid. The local economy, which had been booming when she'd moved there, had soured.

Though way back in the day Helen had worked part-time in her husband's medical office, helping at the front desk, assisting with payroll and billing work, Helen had never really supported herself and she was worried. She began to pinch her pennies and cut back on her lifestyle. Unfortunately, as her social life shrank, the depression and fear she felt when her husband died returned. The golden years felt tarnished.

Unfortunately, Helen's story is not uncommon. I meet widows and widowers all the time who feel lost. Most often, it's the women who feel left behind. They are of a certain generation where they were not the breadwinners nor did they manage the family money. Some widows I've met didn't even know where their husbands left the checkbook. Fortunately, Helen had worked for her husband and his partners, and so she knew how to do something very specific. I see this more often than I'd expect. There seem to be a lot of women in their sixties, seventies, and eighties who did "a little something" on the side back in their day. And even those who didn't do "a little something" in what they would consider the traditional working world were doing more than they got credit for at home and in their communities.

There are many people out there who give away their skills. That's very nice and all, but there are many advantages to actually getting paid for what you do.

People tend to give a greater value to the things for which they pay.

People tend to undervalue, and take advantage of, that which they get for free.

Being undervalued can be exhausting.

Being valued can energize and fortify you.

Making money is a good thing.

Making money for yourself takes the burden off those on whom you might otherwise rely.

Making money allows you to help and even be charitable to others.

Making money can make your life easier.

Making money empowers you.

———

SEAN FITZPATRICK
One Step Forward, Two Steps Back

Sean Fitzpatrick had been a nerd in high school. He liked numbers and math, and thought for sure he was headed to Silicon Valley and a life of developing the next great Internet innovations. And he was. Two years after college, ready to say goodbye to an accounting job at a San Francisco media company, he found the job of his dreams at a small technology start-up. But three months in, the funding dried up and he was on his own again. He quickly found a job tending bar at a friend's restaurant and began looking for another full-time job. Though reluctant to go back to the media company, after six months at the restaurant he was restless and fearful of his financial future.

And he wasn't exactly conditioned to be brave. Sean had grown up in a poor neighborhood, went through an underfunded public school system, paid for community college with jobs in the school cafeteria and student loans, and felt lucky to have the prospect of any secure job at all.

Kicking his technology dreams to the curb and pushing his pride out of sight, Sean decided to beg for a U-turn. After a much-agonized-over letter to his old boss and the HR department, Sean took the first job that opened up at his old media company, this time in the finance department, and decided it was his fate to stay put and play it safe.

Sean Fitzpatrick is a great example of the turtle effect. We stroll about, put our neck out there, and move forward, steady and sure. Yet when the first sign of danger pops up, we tuck in fast, stay sheltered, and hope the world around us changes so we can pop our neck out again and continue the stroll. Obviously Sean had a tough start in life. He'd had no advantages, no access. And yet he had the confidence, at twenty-four, to go for his dream. But the dream shut down on him and he with it.

Obstacles can be daunting. But there are always obstacles; that's the way of the world. As you've heard a thousand times, it's how you face the obstacles that matters. Sean was smart, energetic, and enthusiastic. He just needed some encouragement. I could relate to Sean's background and his experiences. I knew I could help him get a foothold on his finances as well as collect some positive, motivating experiences, so that he could get charged and excited about driving after his dream again.

A New Approach: Playing to Win

As you can see from each of these four examples, there is a tendency among many people to pull in the reins when things get tough. As I said, when finances get tight, the easiest and most reflexive thing to do is to scrimp and save. That is the *opposite* of what you need to do to breathe easier. The best thing you can to do when finances are tight is to make more money.

Saving money, getting fearful, shrinking your life—these are not the way to turn money problems around. I've found that people who take these approaches often stay stuck in their situation. At best they get out of the tough economic situation for a moment, but then soon again they head right back into the struggle. These repeated failed efforts to get on a solid footing can make anyone feel bad and out of control. If you focus on making more money, and making your life bigger, not only will you dig yourself out of your difficult financial situation, but you will propel yourself up and into an easier life. It's about creating the right momentum in the right direction. By focusing on making new money, fast, you will move in the right direction.

The old patterns of acting and thinking about money don't really work anymore. In fact,

**YOU HAVE MORE POTENTIAL THAN
YOU EVER IMAGINED.**

**THAT POTENTIAL CAN MAKE YOU
EXTRA MONEY EVERY MONTH.**

**THERE IS AN UNLIMITED AMOUNT OF MONEY
AVAILABLE TO YOU AND YOUR POTENTIAL.**

**THERE IS NO ONE IN YOUR WAY
EXCEPT, PERHAPS, YOU.**

My guess is that you know deep down, you have always known, that you have a bigger life living inside of you, bursting to break free. You also know that if you make your life bigger, you can have a bigger impact on your family, your friends, and this planet. If you focus on making more money, new money, you can give yourself, your family, and maybe even your friends, an easier life. And you can be an inspiration to others to do the same.

In the chapters that follow, I am going to show you how you can make another $500 to $1,000 or more a month. Think about that. That's $6,000 to $12,000 more a year.

How would that change your life?

What would that money enable you to do for yourself or your loved ones that you can't do now?

How different would you feel about yourself and your life?

And if you feel $12,000 is not enough and that you need more, I know this: If you can learn to consistently make $1,000 a month, you can work your way up to making much more. And so we will start with that: $1,000 a month of new money. When I work with people who want to create wealth, I start by getting them on the path to replace their current income with new money from a business venture. Once I see they can do that, they can leave their jobs, having replaced their W-2 income with the income from the new venture, and start to build something even bigger. But for now, let's just get you to making $1,000 of new money each month. Then we'll replace your income with new ventures. And then we'll get you to great wealth. It's a progressive, straightforward climb.

The key to financial security and an easier life is making new money. There is nothing gained in squirreling away what you already have. Most of the people I know—and know of—who have made a lot of money have spent their time and energy increasing the flow of money to them. They do not focus on decreasing the flow of money out. And they certainly don't focus on saving for the sake of saving.

In many cases, saving is just delayed spending. Most people save to spend. Saving in and of itself doesn't create more cash. Of course, interest on savings can build, and over time, interest can be an incredibly powerful road to wealth. But if you need more money today, right now, you're not going to get it by saving into a smaller life. All you'll have is a smaller life. That's playing not to lose.

HERE WE PLAY TO WIN.

After you read this book, you will realize that this approach to making more money is the single most down-to-earth and practical personal finance idea around. It's so simple your kids or grandkids can do it. In fact, you'll want to get them involved, too.

The time has come for you to make more money, now. The time has come for you to take control of your financial situation.

The time has come for you to build up—and stop breaking down—your life. You know you deserve to live better than you do now. And you can.

Prepare to get excited, because the first step couldn't be more fun. You get to think like a kid again. Get creative. Dream.

TWO

TWENTY-FIRST-CENTURY LEMONADE STAND

The secret to making new money is to take the skills you already have and make a business venture using those skills. That's it. Simple.

But I bet you just hiccupped a bit over the phrase "business venture" didn't you?

When you were a kid, you probably wanted many things: clothes, toys, dolls, models, even magazines. And when you wanted something and no one would pay for it, what would you do? Shoplift is the wrong answer, so try again. You would . . . yes, you know it . . . have a lemonade stand. You'd mix up a batch of lemons, water, and ice in a big old pitcher. Then you'd get the cups, set up a table outside, create a wonderful sign, maybe even one down the road with a little arrow pointing around the corner, and boom, you were in business.

When you were younger, you knew the truth. The truth is that business is not rocket science. In fact, folks have been creating businesses for thousands of years. Yet, all of a sudden, in twenty-first-century America, we treat business like it's something special. Well, as I've been saying for years,

I'M PRETTY SURE CHRISTOPHER COLUMBUS DID NOT DISCOVER AMERICA SO WE COULD ALL HOLD TIGHT TO JOBS AND SLOWLY BUILD OUR 401(K)S (RETIREMENT PLANS).

No. This is a country for and about entrepreneurship, which is just another fancy way of saying making new money.

There are several reasons people believe it is too difficult to make new money and that creating a business is complicated.

One, the most visible new businesses are the huge companies we see on every street corner in every town. Yet those do not represent even a fraction of the new businesses created each day. Most new businesses are small companies, created by folks just like you. These are launched on pennies and usually begin with a home office. And they're all about making new money. Unfortunately, many of these businesses fail because they approach making new money overly methodically, not simply and immediately. And they try to model themselves after the complex businesses seen on every street corner in every town. That's not the best approach. The best approach to making new money, fast, is to keep your business simple, straightforward, and streamlined. As you'll see when you make new money, fast.

Two, the new business products and services we hear about seem superbly innovative, their road to creation intricate and expensive. Or they seem fickle and faddish, like a Pet Rock or a Beanie Baby, their success a lucky lottery ticket. Again, these are the products and services that get a lot of attention. These type of products and services, these innovative business ideas, are not the best route to make new money, fast.

Three, the terminology. People in business and finance tend to use a vocabulary that keeps the uninitiated at bay. And so as the media talk about the latest this and that in the economy or on Wall Street, you may feel you have the wrong education to understand business. That's not true. Business is simple. You have an idea for a product or service, you sell the product or service, you make money. That's how we're going to do it here. And you will make new money, fast.

Four, the paperwork they talk about in the books on the entrepreneurship shelf can be daunting. Forming corporations, writing a hundred-page business plan, dealing with payroll and sales tax, and so on. But this is daunting only if you let it be daunting. Most people get stuck in the paperwork first, and then they've lost their energy to make new money. In this approach, we get into action and then deal with the paperwork. The focus is on making money today. We want that $500 to $1,000 to come in right now, this month. And so we create action and build the company around the action we've already created. There is so much support available to you for creating a business that you really do not need to worry about forming corporations, or payroll. There are professionals who know how to do this stuff in their sleep, and they can help you when you're ready. Too many people prepare and set up and organize first. That may seem the prudent thing to do, but in reality, it's draining and can keep you from even opening shop. In this approach, you will get your business engine started immediately and drive toward making new money, fast.

Five, the time. You do not need to give up your job, or your life, to start a new business. Making new money fast is about starting a simple, straightforward, and streamlined operation that works within the time constraints of your life. For now. If in developing this simple business venture you create a wonderful money-making monster, then you can call me and I'll direct you further. That will be a good problem to have. For now, the focus is on making new money, fast.

Six, you. Perhaps you've never identified yourself as an entre- preneur. You've always gone along to get along, never been a big original thinker, were reluctant to step out from the crowd and do your own thing. That's okay. In this approach, regardless of how you've been in the past, you will realize that you have great potential. Once you read this book, your attitude will shift, and you'll understand how you can make new money, fast.

And So: A Lemonade Stand

The kids' lemonade stand is the approach you're going to take to make new money fast, $500 to $1,000 extra cash a month. Only you're not going to sell lemonade. That's just going to be the model for whatever product or service you actually do sell.

You're going to discover your skill set, find what you're already doing, and decide to get paid for it. Then you will come up with an idea based on the skills you have and the resources available to you. Next you will see if that idea can make money fast. Then you ask for the cash.

Simple. Straightforward. Streamlined. Much like the lemonade stand.

How did that work, exactly? What happens when a traditional American kid embarks on the traditional American kid's business? Maybe it went something like this: The next time your mother went grocery shopping she bought the fixings for lemonade and some cups. That evening after dinner your father scrounged some cardboard and old paint from the garage. He helped you letter a sign, perhaps suggesting what price would be best. It probably ranged from five to twenty-five cents, depending on how long ago this took place and in what kind of community you lived. Bright and early the next weekend morning, Dad set up a folding table on the front lawn and hung your sign on its front. You and your mother made a pitcher of lemonade and she helped you carry it and a stack of cups out to your "storefront." And there you sat, waiting for customers. If the weather was warm enough and your community was friendly enough, you probably made a nice little pile of change. You learned you could make money on your own.

This same story has played out all over the country, for years and years, and is still being played out today. Before it was a lemonade stand it might have been a shoe shine kit. In the fall and winter in northern states it could have involved going door to door with a rake or a snow shovel. Now it could be a yard sale or an auction on eBay. The principles have always been the same.

But as adults, most of us have forgotten that creating a business based on a skill we already have—such as making lemonade or shining shoes or raking leaves—is a viable way to make new money, fast. And we've forgotten that because as adults, we tend to make business, the idea of creating a business, way too daunting. It doesn't have to be. It shouldn't be. You just need a lemonade stand.

Making Money Out of Lemonade

Let's look at some of the things that made business ventures effective money-making tools when you were a kid.

You drew on skills and abilities you already possessed. You didn't have to go out and learn a bunch of new skills or buy a bunch of technology.

You didn't have to invest much money in getting started. You sold something that didn't cost a lot to make. (And maybe even paid back your parents the costs of the lemons and the cups before you took your profit).

You'd seen other lemonade stands. You knew it could be done. And so you copied what you'd already seen others do. Maybe even adding your own distinct flair, like a slice of lemon.

You knew your market. You probably didn't venture far from

the neighborhood. And you knew you were meeting a need that already existed—people were thirsty on a hot day.

You were motivated to make money to buy what you needed.

This is the simple way to make new money fast. And this is the type of business you are going to create. The rules of a lemonade stand are as follows:

- You will create a business based on a skill you already have.

- You will not create a business in an area in which you have no experience.

- You will introduce a simple product or service, already familiar to your target audience.

- You will not try to introduce an innovative new product.

- Your consumer will understand your product or service immediately.

- You will not introduce a wholly original, difficult-to-understand product or service.

- You will be able to provide the service or product immediately.

- You will choose an idea that can make $1,000 in new money every month.

- You will not choose an idea that is not a viable money-making venture.

- You will choose an idea you can begin today, with little or no money.

- You will not choose an idea that requires investment or borrowing to start.

Only about two-thirds of all small business start-ups survive the first two years. Less than half stay afloat for four years. The most common reasons new businesses fail is that they don't start off with enough money. The owner lets his or her optimism and enthusiasm overrule financial common sense. They don't use a team to help. And worst of all, they fall in love with their idea.

The lemonade stand idea specifically addresses these challenges to starting a money-making venture in order to bring in more cash, quick. And no, you're not going to ask your aging parents to pay for you to set up a lemonade stand on their front lawn. You are going to take the elements of the lemonade stand that work so well and update them to today's world and to your current lifestyle.

You will do something you already know how to do. Perhaps something you're already doing at your job. But you will do it in a way that allows you to make new money. By developing this kind of venture, you can generate another $500 to $1,000 or more a month.

By doing something you already know how to do, you eliminate the need to spend time "learning the ropes." There's no need to give up your current job and serve as an apprentice or understudy in someone else's business to gather the knowledge to start your own. There's no need to spend time and money to go back to school to earn a certificate or diploma or license to do what you're already doing. You already possess all the knowledge and experience necessary.

And here's another bonus to this approach: By choosing something you're already doing, you don't need to borrow money to launch the operation and keep it running until it starts making money on its own. Starting a lemonade stand requires a minimal investment, maybe even nothing, to get going. As a result, the cash is flowing into your pocket from day one. There's no need to take out a home equity loan, max out your credit cards, or approach investors. You've already got everything you need to start a money-making venture.

Examples?

If you're maintaining the Web site for your current employer, you can start doing it for other businesses, too.

If you're spending all day Saturday doing gardening and landscaping in your yard, start offering the same service to others.

If you're taking your dog to the park for an hour's worth of exercise every afternoon at four, start bringing other dogs along and charging their owners.

The ideas for money-making ventures like this are almost unlimited. I've put a list together on page 32 just to give you a sense of the endless possibilities. But don't stop there. What do you do at work? What are your hobbies? What are your chores? There's a lemonade stand in there someplace. There are probably several. I've never met anyone, anywhere, who didn't already know something or wasn't already doing something that could be turned into a venture to make quick cash.

Possible Money-Making Ventures

Here's the start of a list of possible ventures to give you some ideas of what you could offer:

Acting lessons
Adult day care
Advertising copywriting
Advertising design
Art lessons
Astrology
Balloon delivery
Bookkeeping
Book binding
Business consulting
Business plan consulting
Catering
Calligraphy
Car detailing
Car inspection
Car washing
Caretaker service
Carpet cleaning
Carpet laying
Ceramics making
Child care
Children's fitness instruction
Cleaning consulting

Closet organizing
Clutter control and office
  organization
Collections
Computer consulting
Cooking classes
Dance lessons
Desktop publishing
DJing parties
Doll making
Dog walking
Errand service
Event planning
Feng shui consulting
Financial consulting
Fitness instruction
Flower delivery service
Food delivery service
Foreign language lessons
Furniture renovation
Garden services
Gift purchasing, wrapping,
  delivery

Gourmet meal preparation

Grant writing

Graphic design

Handyman services

Home entertainment
    installation

Homemaking assistance

Image consulting

Interior design

Janitorial services

Job search consulting

Lawn care

Life coaching

Matchmaking

Moving services

Music lessons

Office work as a clerk or
    virtual assistant

Party planning

Personal shopping

Personalized products

Pet sitting

Photo restoration

Photography

Picture framing

Recording and video services

Review of employment
    applications

Scrapbooking

Security consulting

Shopping services

Silk screening

Snow plowing

Speech writing

Sports coaching

Stained glass making

Tax preparation

Toy making

Transcription services

Tutoring

Upholstery service

Vending machine service

Wake up and reminder ser-
    vice

Wallpapering

Web site design

Window washing

Writing

To uncover your options we're going to do a survey of your responsibilities at work, your hobbies, your regular chores, and your volunteer activities.

What do you do at work?

When most of us are asked what we do for a living, we respond by giving our title. You meet someone at a Memorial Day picnic, they ask "What do you do," and you say, "I'm an assistant manager with Acme Widget over in Centerville." While that makes the conversation easier, it doesn't describe what you do. Rather than focusing on your title, your identity, or your role in the company's bureaucracy, think about exactly what it is you do, or did.

What is your skill set? Do you train people to do telephone support for a software company? Do you make sales calls over the phone and in person for a specialty home product? Do you do bookkeeping and billing for a furniture store? Do you run a magnetic resonance imaging system for a medical facility? Do you diagnose and repair the information technology hardware and network of a midsized law firm? Do you write press releases and newsletters for a major university? Do you manage the inventory of an outlet in a chain of sporting goods stores? The more specific you can be about your work, the better.

To make your analysis easier I've included a "time sheet" on page 36. Keep it with you at work and fill it in during the course of a week. Make short notes about what you did, whether it was "telephoned sales prospects," or "ordered supplies for next week's baking."

You might not find your business idea from your work life. As I mentioned, the business idea may come from skills you use outside of work, your hobbies, or your chores. Even volunteer work that you don't even think about as volunteer work. Most of us have skills, many skills, that we too often overlook.

WORK TIME TASK SHEET

Make short notes during the course of the day and the week about the tasks you perform at work. I've included the weekends for those of you who work then.

	Sunday	Monday	Tuesday
8:00 am			
9:00 am			
10:00 am			
11:00 am			
12:00 pm			
1:00 pm			
2:00 pm			
3:00 pm			
4:00 pm			
5:00 pm			

Wednesday	Thursday	Friday	Saturday

What are your hobbies?

Start with your hobbies. Jot them down on page 39. Don't worry about how often you actually engage in them, or if you think they have the potential to make you some money. For now, just feel free to include all your pastimes. Like to train dogs, but only do it when you've got a puppy? Write it down anyway. Love to cook? Like to take photographs? Make scrapbooks? If you collect tea pots, or like to run model trains, include those, too, even though you might not think them potentially profitable.

HOBBY LIST

Jot down all your hobbies. Don't worry about how often you actually engage in them or whether they can be turned into a money-making venture.

If you're having a hard time coming up with hobbies, think about what you normally receive as gifts from people who know you well. Always getting books and gift certificates to Barnes & Noble, Borders, or Amazon.com? Odds are you're a constant reader. That means you should add reading to your list of hobbies. Receive cookware all the time? You're probably cooking or baking for more than just your own or your family's sustenance.

Think about the things you do to relax, and the things you enjoy doing in your free time. Go to lots of movies? Write that down. Play golf whenever you get a chance? Include it on your list. Love planning and taking hiking trips? Jot it down. Enjoy repairing old bicycles? Make a note of it. Are you an obsessive crossword puzzler? Spell it out across the list. Create as complete a list as possible of all the things you enjoy doing in your free time.

What are your chores?

Next, let's look at your chores. What are the common tasks in your personal life? I've given you a list to fill in on page 42. Don't forget any of your regular jobs or errands. Again, don't eliminate things you don't think have money-making potential. Don't censor yourself in any way.

Make and pack lunch for your two kids every morning? Put it on your list. The same goes for taking the dog for a walk when you come home from work. Create the family's menu for the week, compile the shopping list, and do the grocery shopping every week? Write each on the list. Separate the recycling every day, and then take it to the recycling center once a month? Create entries on the list. It doesn't matter how commonplace or boring the chore; include it on the list.

If you're not able to fill in this list right away, it might be that the tasks are such an ingrained part of your schedule that they've become reflexive, almost unconscious behaviors. To uncover chores you might otherwise overlook, try to jot down what you do every day, during a break, or at the end of the day. You may be surprised to see how much you do.

CHORES LIST

Write down the personal tasks you do, noting not just what you do, but how you do it.

Chore	How do you do it?

What are your volunteer activities?

There are probably some very specific volunteer activities in which you engage. Activities in your community or town, or with an organization with which you or your children are affiliated. But also consider the things you do just as a matter of course in your everyday life to which you don't give value because you're not paid or recognized for doing them. These might include driving older neighbors to the senior center, or helping out in the preschool, or maintaining the garden or playground at the local park.

Include the things you do for charities or your religious organization. If you help with the regular pancake breakfast held every Sunday in the rectory, include it in your chart. If you play the piano once a month at the local senior citizen center, add it.

Charitable activities aren't the only things to include in volunteer activities. Track all the things you regularly do by choice for your social network as well. Do you drive your aunt to the supermarket once a week? Add that to your weekly chart. Is it part of your routine to do home repairs and maintenance for your elderly neighbor? Jot that down, too.

Don't feel uncomfortable including these kind of activities on a list of potential money-making opportunities. You're not going to be asking elderly parents to pay you to fulfill your family obligations. You're just preparing as comprehensive a list as possible of all the things you already know how to do and are already doing.

VOLUNTEER ACTIVITIES LIST

List the services you provide to others. Try to think of all of them, even those you might otherwise overlook as too minimal to include.

Don't worry about writing a detailed explanation on any of these charts. As long as you can decipher the description and your own handwriting, it's fine. If you transport the kids to school each morning and pick them up in the afternoon, you don't need to describe the route, the time it takes, or how much fuel you burn. Just write: "drive kids to school," or "pick up kids at school." Whenever you think of a skill, a hobby, a chore, or a volunteer activity, write it down.

At this point, don't worry about the potential of any task to make money. Just jot it down.

Creating the Cash Community

You are writing down your skills so that you can look them over and come up with a business idea based on one or a few of those skills. If you are in a relationship and plan to make money with your spouse, or even a good friend, ask that person to fill out these charts as well. There should be enough space on the charts for you both but if not, feel free to photocopy the pages. While it's exciting to be self-reliant, it can be very fulfilling to enroll others to help you.

It's important to note that you should be careful to team up only with others who share your positive, can-do attitude. If a friend or spouse tends to be negative, then he or she is not going to keep you excited every day. You want to work with someone who is going to add to, not subtract from, the experience.

For this reason, you may not want to include your parents or relatives in this process. You may find that some of the attitudes you have about money, the attitudes that are not helpful—negative, even—come from your parents. They're not to blame. They are only perpetuating the same fears and myths they learned from their own parents, or from living through difficult times like the Great Depression. When most of us turn to family for advice and counsel on money matters, we receive back the same information that we have already incorporated into our lives and that hasn't really been working for us. For some of you, getting that load of financial fear off your chest means you will need to become a new person: the best person you can be; the ultimate expression of all your power and potential. Family members, even well meaning ones, often want to keep us locked in our historic roles, because that is how they've always related to us. They want us to stay the person they're used to, the person with whom they're comfortable. You don't want to spend time convincing anyone to help you with this process.

You need want to check in with yourself and decide their level of involvement before inviting relatives to help you with your money-making venture.

Speaking of breaking a pattern of negative money conditioning, consider getting your kids involved, too. In my experience, children have a natural desire to start up new business ventures—the lemonade stands, for example. This is also a good opportunity to instill healthy money attitudes in your kids. Help them set up their own lemonade stands and you'll be helping them learn the kind of entrepreneurial spirit and skills they need for success. This is a chance to raise money-savvy kids.

THE BEST COMMUNITY YOU CAN CREATE IS ONE THAT IS SUPPORTIVE OF YOU AND YOUR IDEAS.

Your community can include friends who are always pushing you to improve. It can include teachers and bosses who see your potential. And if you do have family members who fit that bill, by all means include them as well. You're not looking for a bunch of yes-men and yes-women, but you also don't want a bunch of no-men and no-women. You want sources of constructive criticism and support to whom you can turn throughout this process for advice and insight.

Now let's take a look at how the people to whom I introduced you in Chapter One went through these exercises.

MADELINE MATHEWS
Teaching the Children Well

Early one Sunday morning, Madeline Mathews sat down with a empty spiral notebook and a pen to start taking notes for her lemonade stand. As a high school teacher, Madeline's work tasks were fairly straightforward. She prepared lesson plans, lectured, initiated and created dialogue, graded papers, created and graded exams, and stayed late working with students who needed extra help. She coached the debate club and she helped organize Students Against Drunk Driving.

At home she managed the lives of her three children. This meant making meals, buying food, clothes, cleaning, driving, laundry, driving, laundry, driving . . .

Madeline put the pen down, scanned the sheet of paper, and wondered how she'd find a business idea in the list, and the time to do it.

ANNE AND DEAN LARGO
Managing, Organizing, Getting By

One night just after dinner, Dean and Anne pulled out a pen and paper and started their lists. Anne decided that being an at-home mom meant she was a manager, a nurse, a cook, a police officer, a gardener, and a gym teacher. She wrote down the skills and chores she felt went with each of these titles. She also listed the skills she had attained in fashion retail before she had kids. These included a good fashion sense, organization, patience, friendliness, a good memory for details such as inventory and pricing, and the ability to stand on her feet for very long periods of time. She also wrote down her hobbies. None. And her volunteer activities, which consisted of a soup kitchen visit on the holidays, and a few activities at her kids' schools. She wondered if making more money would allow her some time to do a little more good in her community. Perhaps with some of the $1,000 extra she'd make a month, she could hire someone to clean her house and use that time to help someone through her church.

Dean made his list, too. At work, his skills were management, organization, a good handle on operations and flow, and, like Anne, a memory for details such as inventory and pricing. He also had communication skills and felt he was a good representative of the store to the community. He had no hobbies either, except that he liked watching any sport possible on TV, so he wrote that down. But he listed his chores as taking out the garbage, vacuuming, and sometimes doing the laundry. He also fixed things around the house. And almost forgot his favorite, because he only did it twice a year, power washing. He did no volunteer work, but did hold some food drives at the store for several different charities each year.

HELEN GREEN
The Old Days Hold the Key

On a rainy fall afternoon when neither Helen Green nor any of her friends felt like venturing out, she decided to make a pot of tea and think about her lemonade stand. While she no longer worked, Helen listed the tasks she'd performed at her husband's medical practice. It was mostly general office work, scheduling, collecting co-pays, organizing charts, helping with some payroll and billing. Despite feeling financially constrained, Helen still pursued a number of hobbies. The local bridge club had tournaments in which she participated, and she and her friends went to the movies and free concerts in town as often as possible. Helen was also an obsessive reader and participated in two book groups. Ever since her husband died, her list of chores had shrunk. She still cooked and cleaned, but for one person in a condo, neither took much time.

She shopped regularly, went to the beauty salon, and spent three hours a day, four days a week, volunteering at a local hospital. Mostly she transported patients via wheelchairs, though she sometimes filled in at the reception desk.

SEAN FITZPATRICK
Doing What He Can

Sean met up with one his friends at the gym to work out. Afterward, sitting on the curb outside, drinking their protein shakes, they talked about Sean's skills. Sean knew he could do anything technical, including writing software, graphic design, and fixing computers. He'd been a bartender, which required skills of organization and communication. He'd been an accountant, and was detail-oriented and good with numbers. And now he was doing finance at his company, which in this case meant evaluating potential acquisitions for the media company. This was analytical and also required communication skills.

He also liked to work out, a lot. And thought he'd be good at training someone else to work out. Sean's friend reminded him that he'd made T-shirts with clever little slogans in high school and sold them at events. Sean wondered if this would be his—as we say—fastest path to cash.

I decided to have a little chat with Sean.

Loral's Coaching Clip

"You want to be a high-tech guy, right, Sean?" I asked. "Working in Silicon Valley?"

"Yes," Sean said. "That's the idea."

"And how will it help you to make $500 to $1,000 extra cash a month?" I asked. "Why don't you just go get that job in Silicon Valley?"

"Well, it's not that easy right now," he said. "And I'd like to make more money every month to give myself a little cushion. Then when I'm ready to quit my job again, I have some cash to fall back on if I don't get a good position at a start-up."

"I think you're undervaluing yourself and your potential," I said straight out, as I tend to do.

He cocked his head, unsure. Then he shrugged; maybe he was.

"I think you have a big brain and if you had some big guts, you could have your own high tech start-up one day, instead of hoping to get in on someone else's."

"That would be nice."

"And so I think you need to focus on doing something technical, not making T-shirts, to get make more money, right now."

"Why?"

"Because I want you to learn business fast. If you build a business on a skill set you already have, instead of on a product idea you have, then you can focus on the business, the management, the marketing, and learn while you're making good money every single month. If you sell T-shirts, you won't be learning about the customer you eventually want to sell to, you won't be working in the industry you eventually want to be in, you'll only be making money and you won't be learning anything."

"I have to think of a business venture, based on my skills, my technical skills, with which I can make money tomorrow?"

"Or today," I said.

––––––––

Though some people find it hard to focus on just one skill, some are lucky to have many skills to choose from. And from these, they can come up with many business ideas. In Sean's case, since I knew he dreamt of working for a start-up, I wanted to encourage him to start thinking about that in a new way. To dream bigger. To actually believe that some day, he wouldn't work for a start-up. He'd create one. By working on a skill set he already had, one that also might fuel his bigger dreams, Sean would be propelling himself to a brighter future.

Skills in Hand, Idea at the Ready

I bet you already have an idea about what you can do. Just thinking about it may have already given you an idea for a money-making venture. As you can see from these examples, some people have skills that will naturally lend themselves to business ideas. Others may need to dig a bit deeper into the process. If that's the case for you, that's all right. Just make sure you go through the skills exercises as thoroughly as you can. I know that you already know how to do something that can help you make $500 to $1,000 of extra cash every month. And you might even know what you could do, but you've never acted on it. The purpose of the exercises in this chapter is to come up with as many skills as you can. Then you'll have a lot of material to work with when you try to generate your idea for a business venture that will be your fastest path to cash.

As you can probably see already, this approach to money is about growth. You are capable. You have potential. Your life can get better just by using what you already know how to do and turning it into cash.

Not long ago I was where you are right now, so I understand. I was nervous about relying on my skill sets to make more money and I was afraid of wasting my time and energy—and maybe some money—in order to do that. And I wasn't so sure I could change my relationship with money.

But I did. I applied this simple approach to making more money, fast, and now I teach it to others who are doing it every day. You can do it, too. You will make more money. You will turn your life around.

But first, we need to come up with ideas for your money-making ventures.

THREE

DISCOVER THE IDEA

It's time to start thinking of ideas based on the skills you already have, that will create your fastest path to cash. If you think you're moving fast, you're right. That's the goal. We're going to whip through each of these chapters and get into action as soon as possible. It's much better to learn while in action than it is to sit and think. In-action learning is good learning. Experience beats theory every day of the week. Once you've come up with some ideas, we'll move to Chapter Four to examine whether your ideas are good ideas or actually great make-money-fast ideas. We're going for great make-money-fast ideas.

Again, the name of the game is moving forward, so we don't want to spend too much time on any one exercise, even coming up with a good idea. Read through these pages and start writing down your ideas as soon as they pop into your head. Don't filter your thoughts. Let them flow. It will be helpful to have as many ideas as possible from which to choose. This is not a three-week exercise. Consider devoting just forty-five minutes to reading this chapter and writing down your ideas. We're going to go, go, go.

Drawing Upon Your Skills and Resources

Check in with the charts you filled in for Chapter Two, those listing skills, hobbies, chores, and volunteer work. Make sure that your idea is based on what you already know how to do. If you are a good manager and have great organizational skills, but have chosen a business that requires some creativity, like cake decorating, you might not be able to handle the actual decorating part of the job. On the other hand, if you are creative, but lack management and organizational skills, you might not be able to manage making the cakes for three different parties in one weekend. Consider all the tasks and the skills necessary for your idea, and make sure they are in line with what is available to you.

You also want to make sure that you have the necessary resources. Too many small businesses fail because they don't start off with enough money to set up the business and keep it going until it starts taking in more than it spends. Lemonade stands work because they do not require a lot of start-up money *and* they generate profits right away. Money is already tight, so the last thing you need is to spend more—or worse yet, borrow more—to set up a business. What you need is a business that requires almost no cash outlay to get going.

Turn to page 58. There you'll find a chart titled Resource Checklist. On the left of the page start listing all the things

you'll need to run your business. Be as specific as possible, dig-
ging down into the nitty-gritty details. If you'll be setting up a
lawn-mowing business you'll need a mower, a trimmer, a rake,
and a leaf blower, but you'll also need a vehicle to get around, a
cell phone so you can be reached throughout the working day,
and an answering machine at home. If you'll be doing office
work for small businesses, you'll need a computer, a telephone,
a printer, a fax machine, a copier, maybe a scanner. You want to
make sure you already own these things, or that for the first few
months you can borrow them from someone really supportive. At
some later point, you will want to check your Fast Cash Formula
to see when you can pay a fee for using these things or buy them
for yourself. But at first you want access to inexpensive resources
that can create immediate money.

RESOURCE CHECKLIST

List all the things you'll need to run your money-making venture. Then check off what you already have. Make note of any special resources you have that could really help in starting and running this money-making venture.

Resources Needed	Do I have?

Once you've come up with a comprehensive list of what you need, check off whether or not you already have it. On the bottom of the page, make note of any special resources you have that could really help in starting and running this business. This could include other people who want to help you. Maybe your spouse has a skill, such as tax preparation, that would eliminate the need for you to hire outside help.

THE FASTEST PATHS TO CASH ARE IDEAS FOR WHICH YOU ALREADY HAVE EVERYTHING YOU NEED.

However, don't automatically throw out an idea for which you don't currently have all the resources. Try to figure out exactly how much it will cost you or how long it will take to fill in the gaps. It's important to decide if these costs are doable or prohibitive for your money-making goals. If the gap feels a bit too large, consider a sharing arrangement with other members of your cash-creating community.

You don't have to love it to live it.

Many people find that they can do something they really enjoy with their skills. Others find that they have to consider something they can do but don't necessarily love. Consider the following conversation I had with a cafeteria cook named Max who attended one of my workshops. He'd been working in one of the cafeterias at a large university for twenty years.

Loral's Coaching Clip

"I'm tired of cooking," Max said.

"Have you ever made money any other way?" I asked him.

"No," he said. "I got a degree in nutrition and I've been trying to keep the youth of America healthy for two decades now."

"Do you really hate cooking, or is it that you don't know how to make money doing it?"

"I make money doing it," he said.

"A salary," I countered.

"Right," he said. Sometimes I want to create a new class called Workshops for the Stubborn. Max and I had to work to solve the *right* problem.

"You have the ability to make a lot more money with your skills," I said. "You don't have fixed potential; why do you accept a fixed income?"

"How can I make more money with my skills?" he said.

"What do you do as a cook? What are your skills?"

"I focus on health and nutrition. I plan the weekly menus, procure the food, and oversee the preparation and cooking. Then I present it and the kids take what they want."

"Do you think you could do this for another market, outside of your work?"

He shrugged. "I'm not committed to make new money right now," Max said. Okay, so he didn't actually say that. But that's what I read from his shrug. Of course Max wanted to make new money, especially if it could be fast and simple.

"There are several cafeterias on campus, right?" I asked. Max nodded. "Is yours distinct?"

"Yeah, it's popular."

"Why?"

He knew this answer right away. "Healthy options."

"Fantastic," I said. "You have skills and a distinction. Now, can you think of any other market that would like to have healthy options for lunch?"

"The public schools in town do okay. I mean, they have their own cafeteria staff," he said.

"Forget the school systems," I said. "Those are too difficult to get into. Think outside of your job, Max. Think of your skills. You're not a school cook, you're a cook who offers healthy options for kids. What if you offered nutritional coaching to mothers of young children? Maybe put a flyer up for a weekly seminar where you helped parents plan their weekly menus. And you talked about ingredients, balance. Called it Max's Motivational Lunchtime Mix."

Max's eyes lit up. "I could do that."

"Of course," I said. "And it would only be a few extra hours a week."

"But I still don't think that's going to make me any less tired of cooking," he said. "I don't want to do something I hate."

"You don't have to choose something you love to make money," I said. "You don't see a lot of rich poets out there, do you? You obviously chose to study nutrition because it interested you. You became a cook because you had the skills to get a job as a cook. Or you learned on the job. Whatever it was that attracted you to the job in the first place is still inside you. The reason you're tired is because you get paid the same old salary to do the same old thing. Believe me, if you had a money-making venture that was pulling in $500 to $1,000 a month, you'd be a lot more excited about those skills."

"How about a restaurant?" Max said. "That I'd like to do."

This is the leap that makes fast money, slow. "The plan is to make extra money fast," I said. "You can't create a restaurant and make money fast doing that. Let's start with making some fast money educating parents on nutrition. Then, once you learn how to get out there and ask for the cash, we'll look into your bigger dreams."

———————

Too many people think they hate their skills. What they really hate is their job. Whether you like that job now or not, your skills, as well as your natural propensities and abilities, were the most likely reasons you went into that job. And you've made money using those skills. This means that the way you have used your skills in the past is the number one indicator for how you can make more money fast, right now.

Unfortunately, over the course of many years, for most people the job has become their identity, part of their personality. In order to adjust your income potential, you need to adjust your identity. In this process, you will become who you want to be and can be.

Max needed to identify anew as an excited person who knew how to create a money-making venture using his cooking skills, rather than sit in his story of being a cafeteria cook. This alone, this repositioning of his self, would wake him up. When Max begins to pull in thousands of new dollars every year, he won't be tired anymore.

Consider your personality.

When you consider your business, it's also important to consider your personality. If you like details and not the big picture, consider an idea that will thrive on your ability to dig into the details. If you are super friendly and outgoing, look into an idea that has you out there with other people.

Of course, we all know ourselves a little bit. But there are gaps in self-awareness. For most everyone. If you're not sure about your personality, your propensities, your attitudes, or your behaviors, and what type of business venture would work well with them, consider talking to someone who knows you well. It could be a spouse, a friend, a parent, or even your children. The key is their willingness and ability to be honest with you. Tell them your idea for a lemonade stand and ask if they think you have the personality to succeed in that business. Can they see you doing the work well? Do they think you would enjoy it? Don't forget, you're not looking for work that fulfills your life's dreams. You just want to know if you can do it. On page 64 I've included a section called Personality Notes for you to jot down their comments. (If you're going to be testing a number of different ideas, make several copies of this page, one for each idea.)

PERSONALITY NOTES

Tell someone who knows you well about your idea for a lemonade stand and ask if they think you have the personality to succeed in that business. What are their comments?

Think back over your past and see if you can come up with a time when you did the kind of work you're considering. Your past always contains excellent clues to your future. If you realize an idea doesn't fit your personality, don't test it any further. Dump it, pick another from your lists, and start the testing process over.

————

MADELINE MATHEWS
The Obvious Choice

The lightbulb snapped on. Of course. Tutoring. After making her list of skills, tasks, hobbies, and chores, Madeline realized that she could generate fast cash by offering tutoring services. For years she'd been helping students who were having difficulty in their classes after school. She decided the best way for her to generate fast cash was to charge for the kind of tutoring she was already doing on a voluntary basis. She considered a few other ideas, including a Debating Club expo for which she could charge entry fees, tickets, and sponsorships, but decided to hold off on this one for a later date. Madeline felt that her fastest and easiest path to cash was tutoring. Madeline made a good choice. She took a skill she had—guiding students who needed extra help—and chose to do it for money after school and on the weekends.

The next day Madeline spread the word among her colleagues that she was available for tutoring work. A few said they had some students who needed help and would pass the information along when they got a chance. Two days later Madeline received a call from the mother of an eighth grader who was looking for someone to help her son improve his grades in English and social studies. That was easy.

Between those two events, Madeline took time to consider if the idea fit her skills and resources. Madeline knew she had the skills. And she decided that she would have the students meet her in her classroom, during scheduled appointments right after school, so that the travel would be minimal. She would make sure not to overschedule so she could get home to her children not long after they got home from school. For students who had after-school activities or sports, she already had a key to her classroom and she could arrange to meet them another time. The local library in the center of town also had rooms available free of charge, and she would consider using those, too. She also had all the material resources necessary for the tutoring business since she'd rely on the study guides and notes available in her school. Her own, and her children's, Internet expertise could also be a big help, maybe even setting up ways for her to do online tutoring.

Madeline believed, too, that the venture fit her personality and her life. She was an energetic and enthusiastic teacher. She was good with kids and had a lot of experience with both them and the subject matter. She also realized that as a teacher, she was on the same schedule as her potential customers. And she felt that twelve hours a month would not take her away from her kids too often.

———

I liked Madeline's plan. She was going to create a fast money-making venture using a known skill set. It wasn't a big leap, and I knew she'd make some extra money fast.

————

ANNE AND DEAN LARGO
Uncovering the Obvious—A Chore No Longer

I checked in with the Largos to see what ideas they were knocking about.

Loral's Coaching Clip

Dean came up with his idea first. "I'm thinking I can do some handyman work for other people. On weekends, at night. You know, fix things and such."

Anne nodded. "I'm going to turn people's closets into retail stores."

"What do you mean?" I asked.

"I read an article about a woman who sold her old clothes, right out of her closet. She lined them up by size, color, type, and people came to her house and bought them."

"I don't want people coming to our house," Dean said.

"I'm not selling my clothes, Dean. I'm going to help other people sell theirs. I'll be like one of those people who organizes estate sales. Only I'll do it for people when they are still alive."

I asked them if they thought these ideas fit their personality.

"Definitely," Anne said.

"Sure," Dean said.

I looked at him. "Are you sure that being a handyman fits in with your full-time job? You already do a lot of customer service. When someone needs something fixed at their house, they can be pretty demanding."

"Huh," Dean said. "You know what, you're right. I need something a little more mindless."

"How about the power washer?" I asked.

Dean's eyes lit up. "Really?"

"Absolutely," I said. "It's equipment you have sitting in your garage, that you use only twice a year, so it's available. Usage costs nothing, since you own it, and you use the customers' water and electricity. And it costs a lot less to have a house and fence power-washed than painted. And sometimes it looks just as good."

"And they can't talk to me, it's too loud."

"There you go."

We decide together that, yes, they had the skills and resources they needed. Anne was organized, she knew fashion, retail, and felt she could market to the end consumer as well as her customer. Dean knew how to handle the power washer, and he thought he could manage well the selling and closing relationships with each customer.

Anne and Dean were happy with their ideas. The question would be, would they make money fast?

HELEN GREEN
Back to Doing What She Did Best

Helen Green didn't see how any of her hobbies or chores could be turned into ideas for a lemonade stand. She loved bridge, but she wasn't a gambling kind of gal. Her cooking was rusty; she only made a big home-made dinner when her kids and grandkids visited for the holidays. Helen enjoyed volunteering at the local hospital, but that just involved pushing wheelchairs around. However, it was at the hospital where she finally came up with an idea.

Helen was outside the front doors of the hospital, waiting with a discharged patient, when a familiar face walked up. It was one of her husband's old partners from the medical practice. The conversation turned to the role Helen used to play in the office and he mentioned that his niece was starting a small business and could use that kind of personal assistance in her office. The two exchanged phone numbers, promising to get together for lunch.

Later that afternoon, on her drive home from the hospital, Helen began to think about the conversation. Rather than going to work for someone in their office, even part-time, why not start a business as a virtual assistant for a few different start-ups or small companies? When she got home, Helen thought about the idea.

The idea of being a personal assistant played to her strengths—being detail-oriented, polite, organized, and easy to work with—and from past experience, Helen knew that what she needed to do the job was a desk, a computer, Internet access, word processing and financial software programs, a printer, a fax, and a telephone, all of which she had. Helen's time was her own so she could devote herself to the venture whenever needed. While she wasn't as spry as she used to be, the job wouldn't be physically demanding.

The next morning Helen called the doctor and asked for his niece's phone number. She'd look at the idea to see if it was profitable, and then she'd make the call.

————

SEAN FITZPATRICK
Finding His Path

After our coaching session, Sean made a decision. He wanted to do something with his technical skills. He decided that he'd create Web sites. But after some research, he lost interest in that idea. Though people wanted Web sites in his area, a hotbed of Internet creation, there were thousands of suppliers, many people just like him, trying to make some extra money. And they were charging about $60 an hour to do it. Sean didn't like the idea that he'd have to work six to seven hours a week to make his goal of $250 extra a week.

During his research, though, Sean came across another business. There were two companies, one a huge national chain, and one a local mom-and-pop shop, that offered services to clean and speed up computer operating systems. Sean latched onto this immediately.

Sean liked the idea of doing a quick fix and not establishing an ongoing relationship with the client. He also liked that,

unlike with Web sites, the customer would have little or no
input. He knew operating systems like the back of his hand. He
had a viral cleanup disk he'd created with a friend in high school.
Also, he knew most people already had programs on their computer to speed up the pace, but they just didn't—or didn't know
how to—run them.

Sean had a motor scooter, so he knew he could get anywhere
around San Francisco within thirty minutes, and he wouldn't
have difficulty finding parking.

Sean's business venture had the makings of a good make-money-
fast idea. I was glad he decided to drop the Web design business.
Though I have several clients who make a lot of fast extra money
in that arena, I did not feel that Sean had the personality for
this type of work. Plus, cleaning up and speeding up operating
systems on computers was the type of work that related more
directly to Sean's skill set.

I'm always impressed, but never surprised, with how quickly
people come up with their ideas. Just like a lemonade stand is an
obvious idea for a kid in need of new sneakers, a business venture
for anyone who wants to make more money really can be second
nature. If they just get out of their own way, and do it.

Not everyone is going to be able to come up with an idea
based on something they enjoy, like Anne and Dean Largo or
Sean Fitzpatrick. Some people are going to have to return to work
they used to do, like Helen Green, or take something they've
been doing for free and start doing it for money, like Madeline

Mathews. That's all right. This isn't about doing something that makes you feel good; it's about putting more cash in your pocket. Empowerment will come from seeing how quickly and easily you can make more money, and how that can quickly start to turn your life around. You are going to become a new person with a new attitude when you have mastered making new money.

With an idea in hand, quickly examined, you're ready to test if that idea is, indeed, your fastest path to cash. In other words, how many days is your walk to the bank?

FOUR

THE FAST CASH FORMULA

"Loral, I've come up with a great idea!"

I hear that a dozen times a day, at every seminar I run. The person is bursting with excitement. They're wearing a grin that stretches from ear to ear, proud as can be, sure they've found the key to turning their life around. The idea comes bursting out at high speed, with emphasis on the elements the hopeful entrepreneur finds the most exciting. Audience members start unconsciously nodding in encouragement. Then everyone turns to look at me . . . and I rain on the parade. Not because it isn't a great idea. It's just that great ideas are not what this conversation is about. This conversation is about figuring out your fastest path to cash.

Remember, that's our goal here: putting more money in your pocket as quickly as possible. You might have a brilliant idea for, let's say, a new product to clean large screen televisions. Your screen cleaner may be amazing, but if it takes years to get to market, it's not a make-money-fast idea.

Making Money Fast

The goal is to make $500 to $1,000 a month or more. The next step in considering your idea is to examine the Fast Cash Formula, which determines your profitability.

This is the Fast Cash Formula: 12/4/5.

12—Decide how much money you want to make each month of the year.

4—Divide that monthly number by the four weeks in a month, to see how much you need to make a week to hit that monthly target.

5—Divide that number by five working days a week, to see how much you need to make a day to reach that weekly target.

The Fast Cash Formula, like all things in this approach, is simple and straightforward. You'll see this when you go through the chart on page 76 to do the model.

The best way to begin a profit model is to come up with your goals. On the first line, write your monthly money goal. We're aiming for $1,000 a month, so pencil that in. Now divide that number by four to determine how much you'd need to bring in weekly. One thousand divided by four equals $250, so that's the weekly target you'll have to hit. Put that number on the weekly money goal line. Then divide that by the days in a week, 5, and write $50 a day on that daily money goal line.

To see if your business idea makes economic sense you'll need to figure out if you've got a reasonable chance to hit these profit goals. Start by coming up with a price estimate. I've found that people stall a bit when they try to estimate how much they want to charge. This is not a number that's set in stone, it's just a guess. In fact, I'm going to suggest you play with that price a bit later on, so go ahead and put your best estimate there, and don't sweat over it; it will change. Go online and get a quick price using an Internet search for comparisons. Take out the Yellow Pages and make a phone call or two to businesses selling similar products or services. Or stop by a store and survey their prices. Again, you're not carving this number in stone, just using it for some quick analysis. Using the estimated price, calculate how many hours you'd have to work each day or each week, or how many products you'd have to sell each day or each week, in order to make $1,000 a month.

THE FAST CASH FORMULA: 12/4/5

What is your monthly money goal?

Monthly Money Goal: $ _____

Divide by 4 (number of workweeks) for a

Weekly Money Goal: $ _____

Divide by 5 (days in a workweek), your

Daily Money Goal: $ _____

What you will charge per product or unit,

for the service, or unit of time?

Price Estimate: $ _____

Fill in this equation if X is the number of units, services, or hours to reach your monthly goal:

Monthly Money Goal/Price Estimate = X

(for example: $1,000/$25 an hour = 40 hours a month; X = 40)

(another example: $1,000/$50 a unit = 20 units a month; X = 20)

_____

Fill in this equation if X is the number of units, services, or hours to reach your weekly goal:

Weekly Money Goal/Price Estimate = X

_____

Fill in this equation if X is the number of units, services, or hours to reach your daily goal:

Daily Money Goal/Price Estimate = X

_____

Can you realistically sell this many products or work this much? If not, find another idea.

Let's say one of your tasks at work is to do Web site design, and you've decided your money-making venture will be offering that service to local businesses. A quick search on the Internet reveals an hourly fee of $60 for comparable services. You'd be running the venture weekday evenings and on the weekend. One thousand dollars a month is your goal. Divide that by four to get $250 a week. At an hourly rate of $60, you'd hit and surpass your target with just one hour a day, five days a week. That's certainly a reasonable goal and your idea for a money-making venture definitely makes economic sense.

But what if your idea is to sell homemade beaded necklaces? You head up to the mall and find necklaces similar to the ones you'd like to sell going for $3 each. Your idea is to sell the necklaces at weekend craft shows, so you'll need to come up with a two-day target. Since you want to bring in another $1,000 a month, that means you'll need to pull in $250 a week, or $125 on Saturday and again on Sunday. To make $125 a day, selling necklaces that you are going to price at $3 each, you'd need to sell forty-two necklaces a day. If that's too many beaded necklaces to expect to move at a craft show each day, then the idea doesn't make economic sense if you want an extra $1,000 a month.

When an idea does not make economic sense, it's important to look at why it doesn't. You don't always have to dump an idea that doesn't make economic sense. You can modify the plan, pricing, or the way you sell.

YOU NEED TO FIX THE RIGHT PROBLEM.

In the case of the beaded necklaces, a three-dollar product requires a lot of volume, and a crafts fair does not present enough opportunity—that is, it doesn't drive enough foot traffic—to sell forty-two necklaces a day. The next step is to find and fix the right problem. Consider the choice of venue. Is a weekend crafts fair the right place? Well, any place would be difficult to sell forty-two necklaces in one day. Is it the amount of time that the seller is willing to work? Well, they need time to make the necklaces, so working at a crafts fair on weekends is already extended time on the job. Perhaps, then, it's the price. If the seller were able to get $11 a necklace, the volume necessary for $125 a day would only be twelve necklaces a day. That seems a bit more doable at a crafts fair. A quick study of other jewelry in the market might find that this price is in line with the prices for other beaded necklaces. Or if it's not, the seller might look at what he or she can do to justify a higher price. Usually this justification comes in the form of a better product or service. In Chapter Seven, you'll see how a distinct product or service advantage in the market can support higher pricing.

If your idea makes sense, that's great. Keep going. If it doesn't make sense, adjust it. Find the right issue, and fix it. If there is no adjustment that makes sense, then throw the idea out and start again. If you're going to offer multiple products or services with different prices, repeat this process for each, discarding any that don't make sense.

Time Out for Taxes

This seems a good place to mention a very important member of your cash community: Uncle Sam. This country supports and encourages new business ventures through several incentives in its tax code. And so it is vital that you support our country by paying those taxes. There are several ways to deal with this, and I'll share with you two choices.

Choice One: Get the business going and go, go, go. Then after a few months, when the money is coming in, find a good accountant (or go to your accountant) and tell him or her what you've been doing. Most likely, since we're not talking about a huge amount of money every month, the accountant will set you up as a sole proprietor. The wonderful thing here is that your accountant will also itemize many of your expenses that support your business, such as gas and maintenance for your vehicle, a portion of the electricity, Internet, and telephone for your home office, office supplies such as software and computers, and so on, against the money that's coming in. As you'll see, the actual amount of taxable income on $12,000 of new money is less than you think.

Choice Two: Set up the company immediately via the Internet and your local government Web site. Get a tax identification number for the business, a business license, and a business checking account. Then, because the tax codes for companies (such as a limited liability company, or LLC) offer more tax deductions than those for a sole proprietor, you may find that you owe very little tax on your business at the start-up stage. Setting up a legitimate company right away is a good foundation upon which to eventually build a bigger business. If you're thinking this way, and you feel this step will energize and not exhaust you, then I highly recommend a visit to www.liveoutloud.com. We have some great advice there, and readily available experts who can put your company together for you in a matter of days.

Don't spend too much time tinkering with the concept or convincing yourself that somehow you'll make it work. Sure, it would be nice to turn your love of making one-of-a-kind boogie boards into a money-making venture. But if you live in a desert and have no Internet access, the idea is not going to take off fast. This isn't about doing what you love. This is about making money. Remember that your goal is to find your fastest path to cash.

How fast is the path to cash?

Examining that path is the next part of testing your idea. The shorter the path money has to take to get into your bank account, the better. Let's look at the two ends of the spectrum.

Many people come up with ideas for new products. Sometimes it's an invention that meets a common need. Or it could be a home-cooked item that family and friends have raved about and suggested would be a big hit if sold in stores. These are the kind of ideas that have been the basis for some of the world's great companies. The idea of an individual inventor or designer starting a business out of nothing more than his or her own ingenuity or creativity is as American as it gets. All of us have, at one time or another, come up with an idea like this. And every year more and more of us think these ideas are the key to financial success. About 485,000 applications for U.S. patents were filed in 2007.

A few of those patents will be the foundation of successful companies for their inventors. Some will end up being sold to existing companies, turning the inventors into millionaires. Most of those patents will lead nowhere. Even the most successful of these product ideas will take a long time before they generate any cash for the inventor. That's because these businesses have a very long and complex money path.

Many product ideas need to be produced. Sometimes, this can mean designing and building a prototype or sample. That takes time and money. Once you have a prototype or sample, you'll need to sell the concept to potential manufacturers, distributors, or retailers, or else manufacture, distribute, and sell it yourself. That means more time and more money out of pocket. It could take years before you actually see any money coming into your bank account. Your dream product can happen. Someday. And by getting a foothold with some financial stability and business experience, someday may come sooner than you think. But today your goal is fast cash. We want to put money in your pocket now, not years from now.

I've found that most fast money-making ideas are services, not products. And though you may find a simple product idea that nets you cash fast, like beaded necklaces at the right price, products are usually not the easiest route.

Let's look at a simple service business—say, house cleaning. On Monday you tell some people about your new venture. That night, on your computer, you design and print up some posters advertising your service. You also print out a bunch of order forms. On Tuesday you put the posters up at the supermarket, the library, a children's clothing store, the drugstore, and the bookstore. On Wednesday you get a call to come the next day to clean the house of a woman who's throwing a party. On Thursday morning you spend two hours cleaning and hand the woman an invoice for sixty dollars. She hands you three twenty-dollar bills, and on the way home you stop at the bank and deposit them in your account. Instead of years, it took just four days for you to go from starting the venture to making money.

Think through how your idea will actually proceed, following the path of the cash through the whole process. How many people or businesses are involved? How much time will it take from the time you start the venture until you receive your first dollar? How long will it take, after each time you perform your role in the business, for you to receive cash? Turn to the chart titled Money Path on page 83, and write down a description of how cash will flow if you turn your idea into a money-making venture. Don't worry about describing it in words. If you find it easier to just draw a flow chart with boxes and arrows, that's fine. All that matters is that you have a chart that shows how long it will take for cash to end up in your pocket.

MONEY PATH

Describe how cash will flow through your money-making venture. How many people or businesses are involved? How much time will it take from the time you start the venture until you receive your first dollar? How long will it take, after each time you perform your role in the venture, for you to receive cash? Feel free to draw a chart if it's easier than describing in words.

We want fast cash. If the money that comes from your idea takes more than a month to get into your hands, drop the idea. The goal, again, is to get $500 to $1,000 of extra money into your hands—and that can happen within thirty days of you closing the last page of this book. If you don't think it will, drop that idea and find another one.

Someone has your customer.

What is the market for your idea? Is it a local service business that will be drawing clients from your town and the outlying areas? Or is it an Internet-based business looking for customers from all over the world? Turn to the charts titled Market Test on pages 85 and 86. Write down the likely sources of customers or clients for your idea.

If you're going to draw from a specific geographic area, get a hold of some of the telephone directories for that location. If you don't have them yourself, you can find them at your local library or online. Go through the business sections of the directories looking for local business already doing what you plan to do. Cast a wide net, looking for businesses which, while not doing exactly what you plan on doing, do something close or related. List the names, addresses, phone numbers, and Web pages of every similar business you find on page 85.

If you're going to draw from a much larger area, turn to the Internet. Use all the major search engines to find businesses that do what you plan to do or something close. Once again, write down all the information you find on page 86.

MARKET TEST

Write down the names, addresses, phone numbers, and URLs of similar businesses you found in your local telephone directories.

MARKET TEST

Write down the names, addresses, phone numbers, and URLs of similar businesses you found using Internet search engines.

Make sure you hold on to this information. In the next several chapters you're going to use this knowledge to help set your pricing, create business forms, and promote your business.

Lots of people, finding no businesses like the one they plan, think they've hit on a gold mine. "I couldn't believe it," they tell me, "no one else is doing it. I'm sure to make a fortune." The fact that no one else is running a business based on your idea most likely means that there isn't a readily accessible market for the product or service. Forget that idea for now. Sure, there are companies that have been able to make millions by developing original products or services. But most have been big, well-financed companies that can afford to advertise and market and shape public opinion long enough to develop a need in people that didn't previously exist. You are not Apple or Sony (yet). Maybe you'll be able to pursue a long lead–time idea in the future, but today your goal is cash in your pocket as soon as possible.

If you find that there are businesses, either in your local area or on the Internet, that are doing what you plan to do with your idea, that's fantastic. That means there's a market out there of available, accessible, and approachable consumers demanding what you need. And you can make some money delivering a product or service to meet that need.

Our case studies looked at their ability to make money fast.

MADELINE MATHEWS
Tutoring For Dollars

Madeline knew from her experience helping kids, and from the parents of students asking her for tutoring references, that the demand was out there. She learned, too, that there was a larger market than she ever realized. Through her research, she found that there were already three businesses in town that offered tutoring: two were franchises of national businesses and one was run by a professor at the local university. Clearly there was a market out there for her idea.

Some quick online research showed her that people were charging $90 an hour for one-on-one tutoring. Setting a target of $1,000 a month, and using an estimate of $90 an hour, meant she'd need to line up twelve hours of tutoring a month. That translated into three hours a week, which she thought she'd have no problem getting.

It was a fast path to cash. Madeline felt that it wouldn't take long for money to get into her bank account, since she'd be collecting checks directly from the parents of those she was tutoring. She also considered monthly payment schedules, so that she wouldn't have to deal with weekly payments.

ANNE AND DEAN LARGO
Power and Fashion, Fast Enough?

I liked that both of the Largos had ideas about which they were excited. We continued our conversation.

Loral's Coaching Clip

"Are the customers available, accessible, and approachable?" I asked.

"I did some research on the Internet," Anne said. "There are a lot of thrift shops in the town and in our county."

We did a quick search on the Internet for Dean's new idea. Four local businesses popped up immediately. We thought two were probably franchises, two independent contractors. That seemed like a lot for the area, so we decided the demand was there.

"Does it make basic economic sense, that is, will it make money?" Dean got on the phone to call a few of the power washing companies we found on the Internet, while I talked to Anne about her business.

"I used the Fast Cash Formula," she said. "I want $1,000 extra a month, right? And so I figure I'd like to make $250 a session and just do four a month, maybe one a week. I was going to charge 50 percent of the total sale. And so I'd need to sell $500 worth of clothing at each of these to make my $250."

"Do you think that could happen?" I asked.

"With shoes and accessories?" she said.

"Now let's discuss your time," I said. "It wouldn't just be the sale day, which could be a whole day. You'd have to go over to their homes and organize the clothes, set it all up. That could take several hours. Then after the sale there's the cleanup."

I could tell she was losing interest fast. We shared a look.

"This might not be a great idea, right?"

"Let's think of something else," I said.

When Dean got off the phone, he was all smiles. "Three hundred bucks a pop," he said. "Per house. And that's just the stucco and vinyl siding. They charge more for like cedar siding, and then there's brick and decks, and mold removal. They're all more. Can you imagine? I can go around advertising 'For 300 bucks, your house can look new again!' Not to mention your fence. Your driveway. Pools."

"The mold thing could be big," Anne said. "That's a real issue around here."

"I do one home a weekend, or weeknight, and we're over $1,000 extra new cash a month, right?"

It was clear they were both getting motivated around the power washing idea.

I then asked them to consider how fast the path to cash was?

"We'd charge them upfront, in cash," Anne said. "Why not?"

"The guys on the Internet offer credit cards," Dean said.

"Well, I say do cash only and then offer certain deals, like, you know, semiannual checkups with 10 percent off, and maybe a referral discount, like if they have a neighbor who needs it," Anne said. Her retail background was coming in handy. As was her experience creating incentives for her kids, I guessed.

"What are the potential roadblocks?"

"Time," Dean said. "Do I want to spend that much time a week at someone else's house? Since I have to work some weekends anyway, it could mean a few weeknights. I mean, a whole house could take awhile, depending on how dirty it is."

"We'll give estimates, then, and charge by the estimated time," Anne said.

"We?" Dean said. Anne nodded.

———

But as you'll see in the next chapter, as they further discussed their ideas, the more they realized what would and wouldn't work. Anne quickly dumped her sell-your-closet idea. It was actually a very good idea. But it wasn't a great make-money-fast idea. Fortunately, she was excited about Dean's idea. And so was Dean.

HELEN GREEN
Making Real Money Virtually

A quick glance through her local telephone directory told Helen that there was a market for the business. She found more than a dozen entries for personal assistants, and there were four temporary agencies offering office help. There were also small businesses all over town, so there was no shortage of potential clients either.

To test whether the idea made economic sense, Helen began by setting her goal. While she'd like to earn $1,000 more a month, Helen decided to set her target lower at first. An extra $500 a month would make a real difference. She knew that way back when, others in her husband's office made $15 an hour. But they also received benefits. Helen called a temp agency in her area and asked how much they'd charge for an office clerk. They told her $25 an hour, and so Helen used that for her fee estimate. To make $500 a month, Helen would need to make $125 a week, or $25 a day. An hour of work a day? She could do that.

Helen believed that the money path was quick and straightforward. Helen would bill the business owners monthly.

SEAN FITZPATRICK
Speedy Cache into Speedy Cash

Sean knew that the national retail chain and the mom-and-pop store both did a steady business in disk cleanup and speeding up systems, but people had to wait a couple of days for service. They predominately took care of laptops, since most people chose to do in-store service. And in those cases, the customer also had to leave the computer there in the store those days. He thought this would work out well for him to come in and grab a piece of the business.

Sean was hopeful that his idea would make money. The national retail chain charged $325 for at-home service, $225 for in-store service. The mom-and-pop asked people to bring in and leave their machines, and they charged a minimum of $65, but $100 more if the customer wanted to back up their work while the computer was being repaired. And, so of course, most people paid the full $165. Sean planned to go to people's homes in San Francisco, and he would charge $250 a visit. He'd need just four customers a month, one a week, to reach $1,000 a month.

To ensure a fast path to cash, Sean would insist on cash on the day he visited.

Once you have uncovered your skills, come up with an idea, and decided that the idea would make money fast, you're ready to pursue that idea. In order to begin, to get your venture up and running as fast as possible, we initiate a little process I call "Replicate and Duplicate."

FIVE

REPLICATE AND DUPLICATE

Have you ever tried to drive a car and read the map at the same time? It's not really safe, is it? But sometimes planning can be a drag, and you just want to go, go, go. At least I do. And so I am forever grateful for the invention of GPS. I love that machine. You get in the car, tap in where you want to go, and ding, it's there for you to follow.

The art of following the route set by another is way underrated. In order to make new money fast, we are going to use the business variation of the global positioning system. It's called "Replicate and Duplicate." In this approach, you find a business that's doing something very similar to what you want to do and then you do what they are doing. You follow them.

FOLLOW THE LEADERS
UNTIL YOU BECOME ONE YOURSELF.

Simple, right? Just like a GPS.

First, you decide where you want to go. For example, "I want to have a business that delivers balloons to birthday parties." You tap that right into your GPS—called an Internet search engine in this case—and look for other balloon delivery businesses. Then you follow the route they've already laid out for you.

In this approach to making new money, we Replicate and Duplicate for one simple reason: Too many people who think of starting businesses never get past the idea and planning stages.

Doing the tasks required to turn a dream into reality can, in the traditional approach, be long, complicated, expensive work. Some people get caught up in finding a location, building up or buying equipment, and creating inventory. Others brainstorm and think and brainstorm some more over a great name, how to brand themselves and the materials they need to market. Then they work the numbers over and over. Spend days working on a forty-page business plan no one reads. And then they find their start-up costs are so high they need to approach lenders and investors for all the money necessary to launch the business and keep it going until they can start making a profit. It's no wonder that faced with having to do all these tasks few have ever done before, many once-hopeful entrepreneurs just quit before they've even started.

Because you have a simple, straightforward, and streamlined business concept that you can begin right away, there is no need for you to do any of the above. You are on your way to $500 to $1,000 a month in new money, and you can't get bogged down in research and brainstorming. But like all good hikers heading into unknown wilderness, you do need a map and a plan. A plan that does not follow the traditional route, but a plan nonetheless.

Don't reinvent the wheel.

As I've said, business isn't rocket science, even though most of us are taught or led to believe it's a lot more complicated than it really is. Another myth most of us fall for is that for a business to be successful, it has to be unique. Again, that's actually the *opposite* of what's true.

Take a couple of minutes to think about all the successful stores in your area. I'm sure you've been to a Home Depot. Well, how different a business is Lowe's? Did you buy your last television at Best Buy, or did you get it at your local specialty shop? The last time you bought a burger and fries was it at McDonald's or Burger King? These examples are easy to come up with because they are everywhere. Smart business owners stick with what works. Successful businesses aren't unique; they follow a pattern.

There is no need to reinvent the wheel. Rather than spending time and money coming up with a business plan, you are going to model your money-making venture after an existing business. You won't actually be duplicating the business, but you will be working off the example it sets. Then, once you model its operations, you'll work to improve it.

In Chapter Four, in the chart called Market Test, you made a list of businesses similar to the one you want to start. To make this simple, let's choose three of these. If you couldn't find three, go back to the telephone directory or online, and see if you can find three. These will be the comparable business on which you can model your company.

There are several ways to approach this research phase. For many of you, it might consist of two hours on the Internet and you are off to the races. For some, you might take a few days or evenings to visit companies, have a company come to your home, and search the Internet. Below you will see a lot of questions and ideas for modeling other companies. This is an attempt to be inclusive and somewhat comprehensive for those of you who want a lot of information before you go, go, go. If you are not a "collect a lot of information" type of person, or if at any time the following seems too much—just skip it. You do not need to do this step. The last thing you are allowed to do, in making new money, is get stuck. The goal is to make new money fast. As long as you don't waste time reinventing the wheel or making a better mousetrap, you are good to go.

Doing the Diligent Research

If you have a digital voice recorder or a little pocket tape recorder, load it with fresh batteries and a blank cassette. If you have neither, get a little notebook and some new pens. You're going to do some research so you'll need something on which to record your observations.

Pick a candidate from your list and approach it as if you were a potential customer. Take notes or record your observations either during or just after your trial R&D shopping trip.

If you start off by turning to its telephone directory listing, make note of the entry's size and location. If the business has a display ad, describe it in as much detail as you can. What kind of artwork, if any, does it use? How big is it? What information does it provide?

Call the business and explain that you're a potential customer. Is your first call answered by a live person, an answering machine, or some kind of computerized voice mail system? What does the person answering the telephone sound like? What exactly do they say? Write down this "Talk Track" as close to word for word as you can.

Are you provided with all the information you need to make a buying decision? Are you asked to make an appointment to come to a location or to have someone visit you? Or are you simply encouraged to stop by any time? What do they ask you? Then ask every question that would be important if you were an actual customer. What do they charge? Are there different products or services? Any packages that could save money? Do they accept credit cards? In addition, ask how long they've been in business.

What information do you have to provide? Pay close to attention to the words they use. Write them down.

If you start off by going to the business's Web site, take in the information: how the site is laid out, the colors, the text. Consider how it makes you feel—that is, are you interested in clicking around, or is too complicated? Follow the links. Your experiences on these Web sites will help you decide how to do your own Web site.

Consider the actions you can take on that first Web page. Are you presented with a buying option right away or do you have to dig down deeper? Are the costs and prices obvious or will you have to speak with someone or visit to get exact quotes? Is there a catalog section or list of services? Is there a sales agreement or service contract? How about a shopping cart? Are orders accepted via e-mail? Does the business accept credit cards or PayPal? What are the shipping costs? Is there a separate educational area? Are there customer reviews or testimonials?

These questions, and a critical eye on someone else's business, will help you understand what type of processes you want.

It's helpful to get your hands on materials you can use, for example, promotional materials, flyers, and display ads in the newspaper. Copies of price lists and order forms, as well as customer agreements and contracts, can be extremely helpful as you move forward.

If you're considering a business where you will go to people's homes, consider calling a similar company for a visit and a price estimate. How long a wait is it for a visit? Do they show up on time? What are they driving? How is their appearance? Are they friendly or strictly business? What questions do they ask? Do they take notes? Do they have samples to show you? Do they bring promotional materials with them? Do they offer references unprompted? Do they give a written or oral estimate? If written, make sure you keep a copy of the form. Do they explain prices and payment plans? As before, try to commit their Talk Track to memory. How long is the visit from beginning to end?

Keep all the notes and the materials you've gathered together in one place. From this pile you're going to create your own business model.

Blending the Best

The purpose of all this research is to gather as much information as you can, in the quickest way possible, about the best practices and approaches others have taken to operating the same type of business. Your goal is to take what you learn from each of your visits and blend the best practices into a package that's all your own.

Maybe one of the businesses you called has a very comprehensive voice mail system that provides all the right options but does so using a computer-generated voice. Another business offers a simple answering machine that's insufficient, but has someone with a terrific voice presenting the information with a very persuasive Talk Track. You could plan on blending the two, setting up a sweeping voice mail system but having your sister-in-law—who has a wonderful voice—speak all the options and deliver your pitch.

Perhaps one of the businesses has very effective Web site mechanics, based around a well-planned home page. Another may be more visually appealing, using less text and more graphics. And a third offers an incredible wealth of information in multiple secondary pages. You might decide to draw on the site mechanics of the first, take a cue from the look of the second, and provide more information like the third, but perhaps by using downloadable files rather than additional pages.

The promotional material of one company could be very professional and slick but cold, while the flyers of another could consist almost entirely of heartwarming photocopied customer testimonial letters. That could lead you to consider a package of endorsements, but put together in a more attractive, uniform document.

One of the companies might have a very simple order form that contains a short one-paragraph sales agreement or service contract. Another could have a detailed order form and a separate multiple-page contract. You might feel the detailed order form works best, but conclude the simple sales agreement or service contract is less intimidating while still being sufficiently protective.

After going over all your notes and the material you've gathered, give some thought to the best elements of each of operations you researched. Turn to Best Practices on page 101 and write down your findings.

BEST PRACTICES

After going over your notes and research, what do you think are the best elements of each operation you researched or investigated?

How does it all fit together?

Every money-making venture follows a process. It solicits and lands customers, organizes and schedules work, and then bills for and collects money. There are different ways of doing this. To decide the best way for you to fit all the pieces of your money-making venture together, Replicate and Duplicate.

Let's say you're starting a house-cleaning venture. Fortunately, you know one of your neighbors is looking for a new house-cleaning service. Instead of offering your services, you ask if you can help her find one, so that you can conduct some research. She agrees. This will help you to see different approaches, as well as your neighbor's reaction to them. You contact three different operations, but two stand out with distinct and compelling approaches.

One of the businesses you investigate seems to rely on flyers placed all around town: at supermarkets, Laundromats, the post office, the hardware store. The flyers are eye-catching and provide tear-away strips with a telephone number. You call the number and get an answering machine with a very friendly voice that simply asks you to leave a message. You receive a return call the next evening around dinner time and have a short but friendly conversation, the goal of which is to set up an appointment at your neighbor's home. The woman arrives on time and seems friendly and down-to-earth. She goes on a brief walk through your neighbor's home, complimenting her possessions and decorating. She asks a few general questions about what your neighbor wants done, but also asks about her children, the pictures of whom she sees, and pets the dog. After a ten-minute tour she gives an oral price quote and says she'll be able to fit your neighbor in on Wednesday mornings or Thursday afternoons. She says she accepts cash or checks when she finishes cleaning the house, and asks whether your neighbor would like her to be back on Wednesday or on Thursday. You both thank her for her time and let her know you will back to her.

Another cleaning business you contact follows a different process. It appears to rely on display ads in the telephone directory and the local newspaper. When you contact them by telephone your call is answered by a live person. You're told the company's employees are insured and bonded, and that they offer three levels of service: basic (a superficial weekly cleaning), premium (three superficial weekly cleanings and one in-depth cleaning each month), and "manor house" (weekly in-depth cleanings). The rep suggests that you take a look at the company's Web site for more information and informs you that the company sends a monthly bill by mail or e-mail and accepts credit cards. He makes an appointment for someone to come visit your neighbor's house to go over the details and present an exact price. A representative of the company arrives on time. She's wearing a tennis shirt with the company's logo and is more professional and businesslike than warm and friendly. She carries a clipboard and fills out a separate form for each room in the house, asking very detailed questions about what your neighbor would like done in each room, suggesting potential extra services such as carpet cleaning, floor waxing, and window cleaning. After a thirty-minute tour of the house, she explains that she'll be going back to the office to prepare a detailed price quote and asks your neighbor if she'd like to receive the estimate in person, by phone, in the mail, or via e-mail. She says she'd prefer e-mail. The next afternoon your neighbor receives an e-mail containing a full proposal, explaining in great detail exactly what the company would be doing monthly, noting comments about each individual room. A price is provided along with a service contract that must be printed out and returned. Your neighbor receives a followup phone call the next day to make sure she's received the e-mail, and a push to commit.

Both businesses have the same basic money path: money going directly from client to business. However, there were definitely two different processes: an informal, sort of ad hoc but warm and friendly approach, versus a formal, highly professional and organized but impersonal approach. Your neighbor shares with you her plusses and minuses on both, and remains undecided.

You take this information and wonder if you blend the two different approaches: provide warm, friendly, personalized service, but do so in an organized, efficient manner.

Turn to page 105 and briefly characterize the process you'll be taking with your lemonade stand. If it's easier, use boxes and arrows to show how the venture will operate.

DUPLICATE THE PROCESS FOR YOUR VENTURE

After researching similar businesses, come up with a process for how your lemonade stand will operate. Write that down here. Feel free to use boxes and arrows rather than words.

Let's see how our case studies Replicate and Duplicate.

_____

MADELINE MATHEWS
Tutoring Tutoring

Madeline Mathews had a micro cassette recorder that her son had given her for her birthday a couple of years ago. She loaded it with fresh batteries and a blank tape and started her research. Of the three existing businesses in her town somewhat similar to her planned venture, two were franchises of national companies and the third was run by a retired university professor.

The first business Madeline investigated was a national test-prep service that had a local facility. Responding to the display ad in the local phone directory, Madeline called the number. The friendly voice that answered—more a receptionist than a salesperson—steered Madeline to the Web site for the answers to her questions.

It was a very sophisticated site. The company focused on preparing students to take standardized exams. The Web pages consisted mostly of text rather than graphics. There were pages breaking down the offerings by educational level and then by specific test. Once you selected a specific test you were sent to pages showing the various course options available, ranging from one-on-one tutoring to small group classes and large group classes. Prices were determined by class size and frequency. The offerings were packages rather than individual sessions. Ordering was primarily electronic. You clicked through to find schedules and courses available in various zip codes.

The business was located in a storefront in a commercial area adjacent to the campus of the local university. The small reception area looked like the waiting area of a doctor's office. The rest of the location was divided into two well-appointed college-style classrooms. There were some promotional materials available in the receptions area, which seemed to be printed versions of the pages on the Web site. The receptionist was able to register people for classes and take payments, using a variation of the Web-based system. She told Madeline that smaller sessions were held in various public sites, such as the library. There was no information on individual teachers.

Madeline next researched the other national chain in her area. Madeline called the number she found in the phone book and got an answering machine giving hours and directions. She found that the company's Web site was more informative, rather than sales-focused, providing descriptions of its programs and offering links to all the locations. There wasn't much specific detail. It was designed to drive potential customers to the physical location. This company offered tutoring in individual subjects for students in grades K through 12. Tutoring sessions were held at the local facility and consisted of groups of three students or less. Prices were determined by an assessment program. There was little information about individual tutors, other than affirmations that they were all experienced and trained.

Madeline drove over to the company's local site. It was a one-story freestanding building in a commercial part of the suburbs, near strip malls and big-box stores. Entering the building, Madeline thought it felt like a cross between a library and a corporate office. A greeter by the front door directed her to a nearby cubicle where she sat with an "assessment specialist." Madeline was told that that her child would be tested by one of the assessment specialists who would then draw up a personalized program of tutoring.

Price would be based on how much tutoring it was felt was necessary. Madeline pushed a little further and found that the fees generally fell between $75 and $100 an hour.

Madeline was given a large collection of glossy promotional materials that were more promotional than educational, with more pictures than text. She also collected a sample contract. She was taken on a brief tour of the rest of the building. It was filled with cubicle-like areas with round tables surrounded by four chairs. Some cubicles looked like they were set up for elementary school students, while others were more fitting for middle school or high school students. The talking track by the assessment specialist centered on the company's proven methods and its track record.

Finally, Madeline called the telephone number of the third local business on her list, a home-based business run by a retired professor. She had gotten his telephone number from the guidance counselor at her school, whose son the professor had tutored for a law school admissions test. The professor answered the telephone himself, simply using his name. Madeline introduced herself, explained that she was thinking of launching a business tutoring high school students, mentioned the woman who'd given her his number, and asked if she could come by to ask him some questions. He seemed friendly, and told Madeline she could stop by later that afternoon.

The professor lived in a lovely Tudor-style home in an affluent neighborhood near the university campus. There were no signs that a business was run from the home. The professor answered the door and invited her in. He led Madeline to his small book-lined study located off the living room and said he'd be glad to answer her questions.

He explained that he did no advertising at all, relying instead on referrals from his former colleagues who still taught at the university. He offered individual tutoring only, and prepared students for the Graduate Record Exam and the Law School Admissions Test. He charged his college student customers an hourly fee of $100 and was selective about how many students he accepted each semester. Since both he and his wife were retired, he was very flexible in his hours. He said he tailored his approach to the abilities of each student.

There were a lot of business ventures Madeline could duplicate. Now she had to decide how she wanted to do that.

ANNE AND DEAN LARGO
Power Washing Power Washing

Anne and Dean Largo were excited about working together on their lemonade stand. Anne felt she'd be able to add enough to Dean's idea of power washing homes, driveways, decks, fences, and pool areas, that justified their working together in the same business. They realized all of the similar businesses were Internet-based. Since Dean was at work in the supermarket for much of the week, Anne would be the one running the online side of the operation. She volunteered to do the research. The next morning, when the kids were in school, Anne went online.

The first site Anne investigated was actually a window-washing site. Though she didn't think this made sense as a direct business to model, she clicked around the site a bit to get some ideas. She liked the photographs, the bullet points, and the easy links. She noted, too, that commercial windows were a big part of the business. She thought Dean might consider targeting businesses as well as residences. She wrote that down. She also wrote down the name of the site, in case they could eventually provide references for each other or work together in a mutually beneficial way.

The second site she went to was specifically about power washing. The company touted customer service and technique. Anne duly noted that the improper use of a power washer could create streaks in the surface or actual destruction of the material being washed. She'd never seen signs of this on their house, fence, or driveway, but she thought she'd remind her husband that his technique would be an important selling point.

The third site Anne visited seemed the closest to their idea. The company offered power washing of vinyl siding, gutter cleaning, and low-pressure roof washing. They also offered service on brick, concrete, and wood decks. Testimonials were highlighted on the site and the company seemed to distinguish itself as a relationship business, offering the services over and over to the same customers.

None of the sites she investigated had pricing. She called a few companies for estimates, but most of them required a visit to her home. And Anne was reluctant to take the time for herself and them. She and Dean had already decided that they were going to take a low-key, do-this-fast, approach. So Anne typed "cost of power washing" into a search engine. To her great satisfaction, an actual survey of power washing pricing surfaced on the page. She realized that there was information everywhere if you knew how to search for it.

The pricing was varied, depending on the specific service. But for now, she saw that Dean was right, two-story houses averaged $300 for the service. Single-story homes were about half that, $160.

Not only did the survey provide pricing, but it gave Anne several other services Dean and she could offer. These included cleaning grease spots off of parking spaces at malls; cleaning bank and restaurant drive-through lanes, playgrounds, grocery carts, even trash Dumpsters. This was getting exciting. She knew, too, that Dean did not want to do any wiping or squee-geeing, so windows, cars, boats, and trailers were out. But heavy farm equipment, of which there was plenty, was an option, and these averaged $100 per service.

The Largos were getting excited about their new potential.

HELEN GREEN
Virtual Assistant Virtual Assistant

Helen Green took out a fresh legal pad, one of the pack she'd purchased at the nearby Staples in anticipation of starting her business. She sharpened one of the pencils from the box she'd bought along with the pads and pulled out the local telephone directory. There were lots of office temp agencies listed.

Helen wrote down the names and numbers of two that had spent money for a bold-faced, slightly larger listing. None had opted for display ads. Neither of the calls took very long. She discovered that these two temp agencies charged an average of $25 an hour. She also learned that the agencies touted the experience, appearance, and reliability of their temps. Helen took note.

Then Helen logged onto the Internet and checked out the Web sites for personal assistants. The price ranges, and what these businesses offered, varied wildly. There were people who just answered phones or made appointments; there were assistants who included dog walking and bookkeeping. And prices started at $9 an hour and went as high as $50 an hour, again, depending on the service provided and the experience of the provider.

After the research, Helen spoke to her friend's niece, Kelly, the woman who was starting her own business. She got a better idea of the type of services for which Kelly was looking. After the call, Helen considered what kind of business she wanted to be.

First off, she was certain that she wanted to be a virtual assistant. She wanted to work remotely from her home.

Second, she would target start-up companies. She thought, from her research, that these offered the most opportunity and best matched her skills.

And third, she decided she would be able to work on billing, managing and paying bills online; communication, by offering Internet research, basic word documents, and creating promotional materials, like flyers; and procurement, helping to set up a home office by purchasing online, and arranging delivery of, equipment and furniture.

Helen found the results of her research exhausting. She put her pen and pad away, and decided to go meet her friends at the pool.

Loral's Coaching Clip

"People don't procrastinate because they want to do something later," I said. "People procrastinate because they flat out don't want to do it at all."

"Yes," Helen said. "It got overwhelming."

"When you say you offer the setup and procurement tasks needed to get a business venture off the ground, what does that mean?" I asked her.

"When people start a business, there's a lot of little, annoying things they have to do. I'm good at doing those things," she said.

"Okay, like what?"

"Like getting all their services set up, the phone, the Internet, and helping the buy furniture and equipment."

"But many small, in-home start-ups probably have those things, furniture and equipment, Internet service," I said. "What, specifically, did your friend's niece say she needed?"

"She wanted someone to set up her billing, do some online research, write letters when she needed them, like to her clients, and make phone calls when she needed to get something for her clients or herself."

"I think you should only do that, then," I said. "You have too many ideas. That makes it difficult to find your customer, and it also will be overwhelming to you. And we know that if it's overwhelming, you won't even start."

"Okay, so what is my business?" Helen asked.

"What did you do best when you worked at your husband's medical practice?"

"Scheduled appointments, sent reminders, billing, and followed up with the patients," she said.

"Good," I said. "That's in line with what your friend's niece is looking for. Consider focusing only on the billing and communications for start-ups."

"I like that," Helen said. "That's simple."

Yes. Exactly.

SEAN FITZPATRICK
Tech Tech

Sean went to the big national retailer, and after waiting in line twenty minutes, he explained to a disinterested young associate that his computer was running slow. He had his laptop with him. The associate finally looked up, his mouth too busy chewing gum to be used for such trivialities as talking, and pointed to a desk nearby, stacked with laptops. Sean was pretty sure the associate was implying that he should add his to the pile. That was not appealing.

Sean then visited the mom-and-pop shop in town. Another young employee sat behind a glass wall, in a small office, surrounded by laptops and desktop computers. There was no one at the cash register, so Sean knocked on the glass. The young employee looked up for a second, then back at the machine on which he was working. Sean told him his computer was running slow, and that he was worried he had a virus. The associate said he could scan it, but he strongly suggested the purchase of a backup system so that Sean could save his files. He said he might be able to get the computer back to him by the end of the week. It was Monday.

Back at his apartment, Sean did an Internet search. There were a few similar services available. He called one of them and discovered that he could have at-home, emergency service that day for $400, but they couldn't guarantee that they could completely eliminate the virus. He looked up the site of another company. The text and graphics were crude but direct. The company offered immediate computer repair, virus removal, and overall improvement and increased speed of the operating system. Each service was the same price, $25 an hour, service in less than three hours guaranteed. But when Sean checked the address, it appeared to be a fourth-floor walk-up in a building he knew to be part of a large tenement in a desolate section of town.

Sean believed he could offer something better.

As you may have noticed, an essential part of your plan is the pricing of the product or service you are offering. It's a fundamental factor in your economic model. You know you want to make $1,000 a month working just twenty-five extra hours a month, so you know you must charge $40 an hour to get there. And it's a conspicuous factor that you'll see when you do your research of other companies.

But can you charge $40 for your product or service? Sure, you can charge anything you want. The more important question is: Will your customers pay $40 for the product or service you are offering?

In order to make money fast, you must understand how to price what you are offering. The price can be very right, if you know how to set it.

SIX

THE RIGHT PRICE

It's no coincidence that pricing, perception, and psychology all begin with the letter *P*.

Okay, maybe it is.

But in business the three are closely linked.

I've found that customers and clients tend to equate quality with price. If something's expensive, it has to be good. If something's inexpensive, well, it might not be of the best quality. It doesn't matter if that's true or not. It just tends to be the perception. On the other hand, customers and clients tend to equate value with price. If something's expensive, it's not a great value, even if it lasts fifty years. If something is inexpensive, then it is a good value, even if it breaks tomorrow, as in "Oh well, it only cost such and such." It's all psychology and it's not necessarily consistent.

Pricing is both a science and an art. And you are not alone in your struggle to come up with just the right number. Huge companies spend months evaluating their pricing plans. In order to give you the tools to get out there and ask for the cash, I'm going to show you the same methods the big companies use to determine their pricing. But since you are driving to make money fast, you're going to determine your price in a few hours, not months. And it's going to be easy. Simple, straightforward, and streamlined, just like everything else in this book.

"What should I charge?"

That's usually one of the first questions I'm asked about starting a lemonade stand. Not "Will my idea work?" or "How do I find customers?" which are more important issues. It's usually price.

Back to Basics

If you go back to year zero in business, price was determined very simply. Someone had a product or service they wanted to unload, someone wanted that product or service. The first person, the seller, suggested a price. The second person, the buyer, offered a lower price. It was a pure and natural market, seller to buyer. At some point, the seller went as low as he could go, the buyer went as high as he would go, a compromise was made, and a price was set. As similar products and services came into the marketplace, prices maintained that middle ground, but were fine-tuned as sellers competed with each other for buyers.

This method of pricing against similar companies, or comparables, is the method used by most companies today. Companies are constantly making a choice of how they want to be perceived in the marketplace. And they use pricing to manipulate that perception. Do they want to price at a premium and be viewed as high quality? Do they want to price at a discount and be viewed as a great value? Do they want to sit in the middle, and present a reliable, steadfast choice?

As you know from your initial research, there is already a range of prices in the marketplace for the product or service you are offering. Your next step is to home in on the price you want to charge so you can make as much money as fast as you can. In your case, that might mean a lower price and selling a lot of volume so that the overall number is high. Or you may be able to charge a higher price and keep your volume or hours low, and still make a lot of money.

In my experience, I've found that most people tend to under-price their product or service. I'm going to strongly suggest that you

Go against your instincts.

The first instinct of most people who want to launch a lemonade stand is to set their prices below those of similar businesses. You tell yourself having a lower price will help you attract customers. But it may also appear that you're not confident your products or services are worth as much as those offered by "real businesses." And, you are not yet comfortable asking for the cash.

Well, you're right.

YOUR PRODUCTS AND SERVICES AREN'T WORTH AS MUCH AS THOSE OFFERED BY YOUR COMPETITORS. THEY'RE WORTH MORE.

Turn back to the notes you took in the previous chapter. After researching others who are providing similar services or products, you came up with ways to make your own offerings distinct. You're going to offer more convenience, higher quality, better service, or something else that makes you stand out from the crowd. Whatever distinction you've come up with increases the value of what you're offering. And people should want to pay more for it. All you need to do is make sure they're aware of the distinction.

It's always better to go after customers who are willing to pay more for something extra than to target customers who are looking for the least expensive option. There will always be someone, somewhere, who can do what you're doing for less money. Maybe the seller is using this product or service as a loss leader, which is a method used to bring people into the store, or onto the Web site, and then entice them to buy other, more profitable offerings. Perhaps the seller is trying to take customers from others, hoping that once they've won those customers over they can raise their prices. Or it could be that they're just unaware that they've priced themselves into eventual economic failure.

Customers who choose a product or service based on price are the least loyal and the most likely to be trouble down the road. All it will take for them to leave your money-making venture for someone else's is an even lower price. Their focus on penny pinching could mean they'll be slow to pay their bills. And ironically, customers looking for the best price may be the ones most likely to complain about not getting what they think they deserve.

A high price can be nice: quality deserves cash.

Interestingly, people naturally believe they get what they pay for. Say you go into the supermarket and see three boxes of macaroni and cheese mix for sale. One is the old reliable box you've seen for years. It costs $1.00. Another box for sale is the store brand. Its package is a bit plainer and it costs $.75. The third is a new brand with an attractive new box that touts all-natural home-style ingredients, offers some recipe suggestions on the box, and even has a picture of the chef with her name and e-mail address asking for your comments. It costs $1.25. Which of those products do you assume is better? Most likely the most expensive one. You decide to take a chance on the new brand and buy it. Why did you pick it over the established brand or the store brand? Partly because it was new and you thought it would be better. But how would the situation change if the third box had the same packaging but was priced at $.50—even cheaper even than the store brand? What would you think about it? Would you give it try or would you instead instinctively grab one of the others? A new brand, priced cheaper, may send the message that it's not as good as the alternatives.

Your lemonade stand is just like that box of macaroni and cheese. Priced higher than the alternatives, with distinctions that are made instantly clear, it will stand out from the crowd and be more attractive to customers.

Refining Price

Go back to the Fast Cash Formula you originally used in making sure your idea made economic sense. Write your price idea on the top of the Price, Refined box on this page. Now take out the notes from your research of similar businesses. Dig up the prices used by those companies and write them down as well. Take the highest of the prices for comparable products or services and increase it by 10 percent. That should be your price. Be certain about your profit model really reaching the $500 to $1,000 per month target. No guessing or hoping. Use the numbers and be specific.

PRICE, REFINED

The price you used in determining if your idea makes economic sense $ _____

The prices used by similar businesses you researched

$ _____

$ _____

$ _____

Increase the top price by 10 percent (× 1.10) $_____

New Price Estimate: $ _____

THE FAST CASH FORMULA: "12/4/5"

What is your monthly money goal?

Monthly Money Goal: $ _____

Divide by 4 (number of workweeks) for a

Weekly Money Goal: $ _____

Divide by 5 (days in a workweek), your

Daily Money Goal: $ _____

What you will charge per product or unit, for the service, or unit of time?

Price Estimate: $ _____

Fill in this equation if X is the number of units, services, or hours to reach your monthly goal:

Monthly Money Goal/Price Estimate = X

_____

Fill in this equation if X is the number of units, services, or hours to reach your weekly goal:

Weekly Money Goal/Price Estimate = X

_____

Fill in this equation if X is the number of units, services, or hours to reach your daily goal:

Daily Money Goal/Price Estimate = X

_____

Let's consider a dog walking business with the goal of $1,000 a month. A quick Internet search found an initial price of $15 per dog, per walk, per day. The numbers work like this:

Goal:	$1,000 a month, $250 a week, $50 a day
Price per dog per day:	$15 a walk
Number of dogs necessary per day to reach $50 per day goal:	3 or 4

Given that dog walkers can walk several dogs at once, the time necessary to meet the volume increases only by the amount of time it takes to pick up and drop off each dog, not the actual walk. And most dog walkers create a circuit that makes picking up and dropping off the dogs flow smoothly without overlap. As a result, higher volume does not necessarily increase the time needed to do the job.

Additionally, dog owners tend not to be price sensitive when it comes to their pets. The common demand is great service, good care, and reliability. It's a relationship business—with both the dog and the owner—and a high price will only imply a higher quality of service, care, and reliability.

Running the numbers showed that by walking four dogs a day, the target could be reached and surpassed. Let's say that further research finds that there is a local business that charges $10 a day or $50 a week, and that most of the other dog walking businesses charge $15 a day or $75 a week. Taking the top price of $75 a week and increasing it by 10 percent ($7.50) results in a price of $82.50 a week. Let's say you round up and charge a flat fee of $85 a week. Factoring that number into the profit model results in the venture requiring only three dogs: $85 × 3 = $255 a week.

By charging a little more than the competitors, you:

a. Create a perception of higher quality.

b. Have a more manageable number of dogs and clients.

c. Spend less time and energy to receive the same amount of money.

Think about that. Walking three dogs about one hour a day Monday through Friday can put an extra $1,000 a month in your pocket. If you decide you can handle six dogs at once, or two separate hours of walking a day, you could possibly bring in $2,000 more a month. That's $24,000 a year. Of extra, new money.

There are thousands of money-making ventures being created by my clients every week. I borrowed some examples of their profit models to share with you, so that you can see what kind of money is available. Each person's goal was $500 to $1,000 new money every month, $125 to $250 new money every week, $25 to $50 of new money every day.

Astrology and Tarot. A young woman in one of my seminars was avid about astrology and tarot card readings. She worked full-time as a nurse-practitioner, but she was so passionate about her hobby that she often gave readings for free. We decided she needed to get paid for what she was giving away for free. She also recognized that there were many people who liked to get their stars and cards read in groups. She created "Find Your Future" parties and charged $30 a person, with the hope of getting ten people to each. She targeted book clubs and suggested they make it a monthly event. She also went to senior centers, sorority houses, high school teams, and drama clubs. She put out flyers in town and an advertisement on a classified site on the Internet. She also sent out invitations via e-mail to women she knew would connect her to other clusters of women. Her potential new cash was significant.

Price:	$30 per person
Average # of people at a party:	10
Number of parties a week:	1 a week
Number of parties a month:	4 a month
Total new cash each month:	$1,200

Music Lessons. A guitar teacher at one of my workshops was eager to teach guitar to more students and make more money. But he couldn't build up his clientele. Finally, he recognized a need in his market that wasn't being met. He knew that many of his students and their friends, especially those in middle school and high school, wanted to be in bands. He came upon the idea to create and instruct bands. He would put together the drummer, the rhythm guitar, the lead guitar, a singer, maybe a pianist, and perhaps others. He decided to charge $25 per student per one hour of band instruction on a weekly basis.

Price:	$25 per student, per week
Average # of students in a band:	4 or 5
Number of bands a week:	2
Total new cash each week:	$200 to $250
Total new cash each month:	$800 to $1000

Catering, Cooking Lessons. Last year, a great woman came to a weekend workshop. She was in her sixties, a grandmother, and worked as a home health care aid. She did not like her job or the old man for whom she worked. She was born and bred in New Orleans, and her dream was to have a Cajun restaurant. She was very charismatic and I suggested she consider offering Cajun cooking classes and catering services to create some new money every month. She priced out the model.

Catering price:	$60 per person
Cooking class price:	$50 per student per class, including a meal
Costs for food:	$20 per person
Average # of parties a month:	1, averaging 20 people per party
Average # of cooking classes/month:	1, averaging 12 people per class
Total new cash each month:	$800 from catering, $360 from class

This was very exciting. With $1,160 of new money each month, she could replace her income from her job. If she worked toward two parties and two classes a month, she could double her income, working only on weekends. She had the skills. Her success would be 100 percent contingent on her marketing efforts.

Desktop Publisher. Though blogs are everywhere, there is still a market and a need for newsletters. One of my clients was very proficient at creating these newsletters. He had created an in-house newsletter as part of his job at a hospital. He decided he would ask a nearby hospital, which didn't have a staff/patient publication, if they'd be interested and how much they would pay. To his surprise, he found out this was worth $1,000 a month to them. Something he was doing at his other job as part of his job was worth $1,000 a month to another hospital. He estimated it would only take a few extra hours a week to find the stories and interview doctors and patients at the other hospital. Sometimes it is shocking how available the new money can be.

Fitness Instructor. A woman in my town taught water aerobics at the YMCA and arthritis chair exercise classes at the senior center. She was a very popular instructor and her classes were always full. She decided that she'd like to try to do some personal training, one-on-one, for seniors only. She knew certified trainers were making anywhere from $60 to $150 an hour at the various fitness centers around town. She wasn't certified, but she thought she'd look into charging $75 an hour for one-on-one, specialized senior training. She would target five seniors a week for one hour sessions, and devote five hours to this every Saturday. She would market her service by announcing it in her classes. The senior center appreciated any extra offerings to their members, and would give her the space for free.

Price:	$75 per person
Average # of seniors per week:	5
Total new cash each week:	$375
Total new cash each month:	$1,500

Foreign Language Lessons. A retired (okay, here I have to use that word) high school Spanish teacher in Miami, Florida came to one of my classes and suggested that she could be a bilingual tour guide for Spanish-speaking visitors to her city. But those tourists weren't as abundant as she hoped. Most visitors who came had family and friends on whom they could rely. We talked instead about the demand many English-speaking adults in her area had to learn Spanish, specifically business executives and managers. She came up with an idea for lunchtime Spanish seminars, sponsored and paid for by the companies. She would offer one a week, on Tuesdays, Wednesdays, and Thursdays at three different companies, for $200 a week, no matter how many students showed up. She did the profit model and realized she could potentially pull in $2,400 of extra cash a month, working three hours a week. Outstanding.

Handyman. An older electrician from the Northeast was bored with no longer working and wanted to find $1,000 a month. He could use it, he said, to support his golf habit. There were several contractors, plumbers, and electricians in his area, but many were very expensive and didn't travel for the small jobs. He wondered if he could make any money charging about $60 an hour.

Price:	$60 per hour
Average # of hours per week:	4
Total new cash each week:	$240
Total new cash each month:	$960

He thought $60 an hour and four hours of work a week were very conservative estimates. He was surprised how quickly the potential cash added up.

Lawn Care. Two college roommates realized they were the only people in their neighborhood who mowed and cared for their own lawn. They asked their neighbors what they were paying for lawn care, and they were surprised to find that it was $100 per lawn and that each lawn was mowed twice a month. The guys decided to send out a flyer offering what they called "continuous lawn care" for $300 a month, which included mowing on an as-needed basis. They promoted their service as neighborly and personal, and cited the green initiative of not driving a big, loud, gas-guzzling truck around and into the neighborhood. If just eight of the sixty houses on their block said yes, they'd have $1,200 of extra money a month. Each.

Recording Engineer. The technology and software in computers these days is amazing. Especially if you know how to use it.

One of my clients spent many of his free hours using the music recording software programs to record his songs. He decided he could create demo CDs for other musicians. He knew most recording studios in his area charged $75 an hour. He thought he'd charge $100 and offer five free CDs, instead of the usual two, since the cost of CDs and copying was minimal. Another distinct advantage he would share would be his musicianship and his efficiency, so the artists' overall cost would be lower. He estimated that most solo singers need about six hours in a traditional recording studio, an hour to get their tracks down, five hours to work with the background mix. He estimated that with his mixing and production software, a musician could be in and out in three hours.

Price:	$100 per hour
Average # of artists a week:	1
Average # of hours per week:	3
Total new cash each week:	$300
Total new cash each month:	$1,200

Seniors' Shopping Service. Seniors need assistance. And they like—and deserve—a little attention. Most of the grocery shopping services are impersonal. One of my clients, a college student in her early twenties, decided she'd provide personalized shopping for seniors. She'd go to their home, sit with them, make the lists, go shopping, bring the food back to their home, help them unload the food, and maybe sit and talk with them a bit before she left. She wanted to offer a service and a relationship. She would allocate two hours per client, and charge each client $50 per service. She hoped they would hire her weekly and she wanted to do this three afternoons, and one weekend day a week.

Price:	$25 an hour
Average # seniors a week:	4
Average # of hours per week:	8
Total new cash each week:	$200
Total new cash each month:	$800

Is this fun or what? Do you see how quickly a small business can make a whole lot of money? I hope you can see that the possibilities and potential are endless.

Go back to your earlier profit model and substitute the new price for the one you previously used and rerun the numbers. Excited by the results? You should be. There's money out there, waiting for you to claim it.

Our case studies made that discovery too.

MADELINE MATHEWS
Pricing Like a Professor

Madeline Mathews's initial research found that the two Internet companies were charging $90 an hour for subject tutoring. She also knew that the retired college professor charged $100 an hour.

Madeline's initial reaction was to charge less than the college professor. After all, he had a doctorate and was tutoring college students to take an advanced exam to get into law school or graduate school. She underestimated herself as "just a teacher who would be helping secondary school kids with their course work." But she also noted that there were companies charging $90 an hour for subject-oriented secondary school tutoring by people far less qualified than she, and this gave her a shot of confidence. She decided to charge 10 percent more than the other secondary school tutors, which, with a little rounding up, would bring her to the same price as the retired college professor: $100 per hour.

When she reran the numbers at that price, she found that three hours a week of tutoring would net her $1,200 a month. Madeline could also set up group seminars online that could expand the venture's model and reach.

Price per hour:	$100
Average # of students:	3
Average # of hours a week:	3
Total new cash each week:	$300
Total new cash each month:	$1,200

ANNE AND DEAN LARGO
Power Profits

Anne and Dean decided they would try the 10 percent rule and charge $330 per house, and $110 per large piece of farm equipment, such as trucks and tractors. They also priced out driveways and fences at $10 a yard. Both Anne and Dean were excited about the idea of doing playgrounds and Dumpsters, but for now they thought they'd focus on houses. Dean was only interested in working about three to five extra hours a week. Their angle was "why paint when you can power wash?" and they also were going to target mold, which was a major issue in their area.

Price per house:	$330
Price per trucks/tractors	$100
Average # of houses a month:	3
Average # trucks/ tractors a month:	2
Total new cash each month:	$1,190

And they hoped this would be just the beginning.

HELEN GREEN
Personally Profitable

Helen decided that she would charge a little more than the temp agencies and the virtual assistants she saw online. Her price was $30 an hour. She marketed her experience, as well as her calm and collected personality, as her distinct advantage.

Price per hour:	$30
Average # clients a week:	2
Hours per client, per week:	3
Average # of hours a week:	6
Total new cash each week:	$180
Total new cash each month:	$720

Six hours of work would be very manageable, and with one client in hand, Helen was sure she could get another. Energized by the prospect of making this money, she called her friend's niece and ran past her the idea of a virtual assistant for three hours a week. "When can you start?" the woman asked.

SEAN FITZPATRICK
Making a Nice Price

Sean set his price at $250 per service and believed it would take him at most two hours to fix a machine. He also wanted to allow an hour for travel each week. He already had a request from the restaurant for which he bartended to come in and work on three of their computers. He offered them a special "restaurant rate" of $600 for all the machines. And he asked his friend, the restaurant's owner, to refer him to other restaurants. Sean hoped to do three personal computers, and one restaurant or commercial business a month.

Price per individual client:	$250
Price per business client:	$600 flat rate for 3 or 4 computers
Hours per client, per week:	3
Number of clients a month:	3 personal, 1 business
Total new cash each month:	$1,350

When you decide to set your prices higher than your competitors, you must make it clear to your customers why your distinctions are worth the extra money.

SEVEN

STAND AND DELIVER

Ythe skills that support your idea, an idea that's been tested to see if it will make cash fast. You have examined other companies, you know the best concepts and process for your money-making venture, and you're set on your price.

The next step is to deliver your message to your customer, to *ask for the cash*.

But before you can deliver the message, you need to create the content of that message. And the content must be more than concept and process you have pulled from other companies. The content must also relay two important points about your company. One, it's different from others, and two, it supports a higher price point. The bicycle is built, now it needs the bells and whistles.

BE SIMILAR BUT DIFFERENT.

There are many ways to stand out from—and reasons to charge a higher price than—your competitors. As we discussed in the previous chapter on pricing, these distinct advantages include:

- Better service

- Extra value

- Higher quality

- Convenience.

You need distinctions that will help you stand out and that justify your price.

Once you decide on your distinctions—that is, where you *stand*—you will relay these benefits to your customer and *deliver*.

Stand out in the crowd: create your distinctions.

As you know, "unique" and "distinct" mean two different things. A unique venture would be one of a kind, the only operation of its type in a particular area or maybe in the world. A distinct venture, on the other hand, is one which is similar to other operations but that has some element that makes it stand out from the crowd. Since you are in business to make money fast, you don't have time to create an innovative new product or service. You want to be distinct, not unique.

Let's go back to that home-cleaning business example. You've decided that it's going to follow a blended approach of efficient but personalized service. But to make the business distinct, you need to do more. One way would be to have a special identity, say, as the cleaning service that uses all-natural products, and promote that to mothers of young children. Another would be to offer different kinds of services. You might offer a special party cleaning option, in which you provide a one-time extensive cleaning timed right before a particular event. Or you might offer special cleaning services for those major once-a year-chores, such as window cleaning, silverware polishing, or even gutter cleaning.

When you have a distinct feature to offer the customer, it doesn't matter if there are five other house-cleaning businesses out there offering their services for a lower price. In a way you are not competing with them. You are offering something else altogether, something distinct.

Distinctions don't have to be big. And in order to make money fast, they probably won't be. Again, it's not a unique offering, it's just distinct. The distinction needs only to provide a benefit or promise that's different from what's currently being offered in the marketplace, or different from what's being currently marketed as part of the product or service. Your competitors might even have the same exact benefit to their product or service, but they never thought to use it as a marketing tool.

There's a classic example of this "creating a distinction because no one else thought to point it out before." Many years ago, a coffee company began to advertise that their coffee was "mountain grown." They even included a mountain in their logo. This made customers stand up and take notice. It sounded exciting, exotic even, and there was an implication that the coffee was fresh. But then the other coffee companies clarified that all coffee was mountain grown, they'd just never thought to make a point of it. The first company never said it was the only coffee that was mountain grown; they just made the point. And it was their brand that was forever associated with this distinction.

As you'll see, it just takes some creativity. Maybe you are going to deliver balloons, just like the five other balloon delivery companies in town, but you are going to do it in a clown suit. That's a distinction. It helps create a specific message—imagine a poster with a clown holding balloons—and it justifies the higher price point.

Come up with five key distinctions for your lemonade stand. When I came up with my financial coaching business, I Replicated and Duplicated what I saw others doing, but I also knew I wanted to offer something more. I wanted to offer personal service. I wanted each customer to feel that they were being personally attended to. I believed that the products and services should be tailored to each client, and promised that no coach or strategist would ever read off a one-size-fits-all script. I also wanted to sell the customer what they actually bought. This meant that if I advertised that I was giving a seminar, then I'd be the one at the seminar. There would be no substitutions for me as the key speaker when that was what was advertised. Another distinction was our desire to provide a step-by-step real action plan to make more money. I'd seen too many programs that were all theory and no action. And I also wanted to create a community so that every positive-minded person searching for abundance felt supported and encouraged, with resources and assistance.

The Five Key Distinctions of Live Out Loud

1. Personal educational coaching service ·

2. Specific, tailored programs and workshops

3. No substitutions for key speakers

4. Step-by-step action plans

5. A community of resources and support

While at first these distinctions allowed me to stand out from the crowd, eventually they helped me create a whole new arena of financial coaching. Soon enough we became the only company that knew and worked with each of our clients personally and as a community. Our distinct benefits attracted a whole world of wealth builders, and we grew beyond my wildest dreams.

And it wasn't that difficult. We just offered the services and products we thought we would have wanted as clients of our own company. And that's a good way to look at it. Consider what you would want, and offer it.

Let's look at the house cleaning example above.

The Five Key Distinctions of the House Cleaning Service

1. Use all-natural products, safe for children and pets.

2. Clean mirrors and wastebaskets.

3. Shampoo rugs every other month.

4. Offer annual "house physicals" that include window and chandelier cleaning.

5. Buyers of a twelve-month service plan receive one month free.

As you can see, the examples of distinctions are endless. But they usually orbit around better service, extra value, higher quality, and convenience.

Let's look at our necklace business. This lemonade stand just needed to fix the right problem. In this case, the problem was price. In order to increase the price, distinctions needed to be created to support that new price.

The seller wanted to justify an $11 price point in order to target eleven or twelve necklaces a day—twenty-four necklaces for the weekend—to make $250 a week toward $1,000 a month. After some research into other companies selling beaded necklaces, it was apparent that the beads on these higher priced necklaces were higher quality. Others were using stones; this seller was using less-expensive wooden beads and did not want to increase the cost of making the necklaces.

And so a different choice was made. Creativity and positioning came into play. To each necklace was added another bead, this one with a symbol on it. Some had hearts, some had dollar signs, some had peace signs. Then the seller wrote up a "symbol significance" sheet for each symbol. Necklaces with the love sign brought love on the day they were worn. Necklaces with a dollar sign were to be worn on days that the wearer needed good fortune. The necklaces with the peace sign on it had special energy to provide individual or universal calm on any given day. The seller also put "symbol significance" posters around the booth to sell the concept before the consumer even saw the actual necklaces.

This type of extra benefit is not as concrete as something like, well, like a bell or a whistle. However, this is more often the case than not. We've all paid twice as much for coffee at national coffee chain than we paid for a similar cup at the local deli. But we perceive the national chain's coffee, packaged in its sturdy white paper cup, to be better. Good-luck necklaces offer a similar intangible benefit. Customers have been known to like the idea of good-luck totems. They buy into the benefit. They think it's fun. And, this seller hopes, worth the price.

Adding a distinction to your business, as you can see, does not need to cost a lot of money. It's about addressing the needs of your customer as efficiently and effectively as you can.

On page 144, "Five Key Distinctions," write down how your lemonade stand is distinct.

FIVE KEY DISTINCTIONS

Write down the ways in which you will help your venture stand out in the market.

1.

2.

3.

4.

5.

Once you have identified the distinctions that help you stand out from the crowd and justify your higher price point, you need to include one more distinction: you. You are your business, and your business is you. And no matter what, the two will be intertwined. When people buy the product or service of a lemonade stand, many times they do so because they trust and like the lemonade stand owner.

DON'T FORGET: ONE OF YOUR DISTINCTIONS IS YOU.

You are almost ready to create the message you will use to ask for the cash. And in order to do this as quickly as possible, you will develop a Talk Track. But first, let's get *you* ready to deliver it.

Who are you, anyway? A new identity.

You are your message. You must feel worthy of selling the product or service you are offering, or else no one is going to stop by your lemonade stand. Remember those enthusiastic kids who waved their arms and held their signs closer to the street? Didn't you think they had something great to offer? Of course; it was compelling. And not because it was hot out or the lemonade stand had a picture of a glass filled with ice and dripping with condensation. No, it was those dang kids.

As you venture out on your lemonade stand, it is essential that you are enthusiastic about the venture. And not just in your room. I mean out there, on the street, waving your arms, holding up a poster.

There are many front lawns in your life. You are out there all the time. At parties, standing on the sidelines of your kids' games, bumping into friends at the supermarket. All of these arenas are grounds for small talk. When you own a lemonade stand, small talk is no longer a chore. It's an opportunity.

A significant portion of small talk always seems to center around questions like:

"And what do you do?" or

"What are you up to these days?" or

"How's the job?"

And most of us answer these questions with descriptions of or stories about our jobs. For most people, a job has become an identity. Identifying with a job has provided many men and women with a substantial amount of worthiness. There's a sense of satisfaction when you can say: "I'm an executive at Blue Chip Inc." But it can be imprisoning, too. Many moms stay home with their kids, but is that their identity? There's always that pang of "Who am I, really?" And what happens to identity when a person loses their job after even just five years? What about the person who leaves the job after thirty years? Identifying with a job can be a great comfort. But when the security blanket slips away, then what?

When you embark on a lemonade stand, that's what you want to become your identity. You are an entrepreneur. You are a business owner. You are a creative, dynamic, and energetic person who is going to create new money, today. And you welcome anyone to do the same. You are empowered. You are inspiring. You are at the start of something great.

In order to buy into this new identity, you must live it out loud. As I said, that's the name of my company for a reason. I believe the conversation we need to have is about the positive aspects of money. Money creates opportunity, gives us a chance to do well for ourselves and to do good for others. Money is not taboo; it's a big part of life and it has a big impact on everything we do.

MONEY IS NOT THE MOST IMPORTANT THING IN LIFE, BUT IT CAN HAVE THE BIGGEST IMPACT.

It's important to have a healthy relationship with money. And having conversations about money with those who share a positive attitude is part of that healthy relationship.

Small talk is a good avenue to begin. When you are in the land of lemonade stands, small talk is no longer a chore. It is an opportunity. An opportunity to identify yourself as the person you want to be, the person you are going to be. Let's go back to our cafeteria cook, Max.

"What do you do?"

"I'm a cook in a university cafeteria," Max could say.

That should be his old identity. In Max's new world, he's an entrepreneur, a businessperson, empowered and inspiring. Max should choose a better answer. An answer that could lead to creating abundance in his life.

Let's try Max, take two.

"What do you do?"

"I'm a nutritional counselor and coach. I lead groups in preparing their weekly meals, and advise them on optimal meal plans for their children."

"Really?"

"Yes," Max would say. "This is my current business. It's great and I love to talk about it. I can tell you more if you'd like."

This is how Max and his new business will grow. Max won't get any business for his business stating his W-2 job. It's necessary to live out loud about what you do, to state your identity. Feel good about what you are doing. Be worthy. Consider the following positive thoughts:

- It is empowering to go into business for yourself.

- It helps your family and friends if you make more money.

- Only people with money can donate money.

- Money gives you the opportunity to do well, and do good.

- Being in control of your own finances helps the economy.

- Money can be used to create a better world.

- Owning a business creates a legacy of financial stability for your children.

- Abundance creates abundance.

Begin to identify as a business owner. When you focus your attention on your intention, you will be amazed at the profits that will flow your way.

Shout it out to the market: deliver your distinctions.

Now that you are ready to talk about your new venture, you need language to do that. We call this a "Talk Track." A Talk Track is some well-thought-out language that confidently and concisely proclaims who you are and what you do for your money-making venture. Some people call this the "elevator pitch." It's that ten-second sentence in which you can explain your business venture.

The purpose of the Talk Track is not only to avoid run-on and confused sentences, but also to prompt potential customers to inquire about your business. If you share your Talk Track often enough, you'll find customers, either directly or through referrals. And before you know it, others may be pitching your Talk Track for you.

In order to develop your Talk Track, turn to page 150 on which you've described the process you'll be following and to page 144 on which you've written down the distinctions that will set your business apart. Read them over and try to combine them into a very short, one- or two-sentence description of your lemonade stand. Think of it as an answer to the question, "What do you do?" When you come up with a Talk Track you're happy with, write it down, in large capital letters, on page 150. Repeat it to yourself over and over until it's second nature. Then get out there and share it with others.

TALK TRACK

In one or two sentences, describe your lemonade stand. Structure the sentence or sentences so that you relay a) the name of your business, b) the service or product you provide, c) its distinct advantage, and d) to whom you provide the service or product.

As an example, let's go back to the home cleaning business. The business process is a blend of efficiency and personalized service. The distinction is using only all-natural cleaning products. These could be combined into this Talk Track:

"I run All-Natural Cleaners. We provide personalized home cleaning services in an efficient, professional manner, using only all-natural products that are safe for children and pets."

Note how that sentence includes the name of the business, what it does, its specific benefit, and whom the product or service is for. Let's visit our case studies and see what they've come up with.

MADELINE MATHEWS
Tailored Tutoring

After dinner one evening, Madeline sat down with her notes and all the material she'd gathered. She began writing down what she thought were the best practices of each of the businesses she had studied—the practices she wanted to replicate in *her* business.

Madeline thought the best things about the first business she'd researched were its Web site and the efficiency of its operation. The second business, which would be her closest competitor, created a pleasant physical environment for tutoring. The professor's home-based business was far and away the least professionally run, but it was obvious that his warmth and personal touch made up for any lack of efficiency. The first two businesses required clients to sign a contract and pay in advance for a set number of sessions. The professor accepted cash or a check at the end of each session.

Madeline began thinking about how she could blend what she'd discovered into her own money-making venture. She realized that she'd need to adopt the kind of personalized approach of the professor, but that she'd add a more structured environment and be more aggressive about soliciting business. To distinguish her business, Madeline decided that she'd focus on subject-based tutoring rather than teaching toward a particular test, and that she'd travel to the students' homes.

Madeline's Five Key Distinctions

1. Personalized service, experienced service provider

2. Subject-based assistance, not test-based

3. Results orientation

4. Confidentiality

5. Proven ability to motivate and energize students

With these in mind, Madeline came up with her first Talk Track:

"I'm an award-winning educator who provides personalized, subject-based tutoring to secondary school students."

Madeline began practicing and speaking this out loud.

––––––––

As you can see, it's not important to list all of your distinctions in your Talk Track. A brief sentence is best. But it must be a *compelling* brief sentence. The goal is to initiate a conversation. When someone asks Madeline "What do you do?" she has a quick answer. Then the follow-up conversation can include the other benefits of hiring her as a tutor. Most people do not like to be overpitched or oversold. Enrollment is the key. You want to enroll and engage potential customers in a conversation by getting their attention with a quick teaser sentence. That's your Talk Track.

ANNE AND DEAN LARGO
Powered Up for Power Washing

Anne discussed her initial research with Dean. He too got excited, and thought their power washing idea was doable.

Anne and Dean's Five Key Distinctions

1. A fresh idea in home improvement

2. A mom-and-pop operation in the neighborhood

3. Efficiency and effectiveness

4. Neighbor-to-neighbor referral discounts

5. Satisfaction guaranteed

They were eager to get started right away. They had many ideas on how to ask for the cash. But first they needed to work on their Talk Track. They came up with:

"Why paint when you can power wash? Power washing
is an inexpensive, highly effective way to make your
home, fence, or driveway look fresh and new again."

The Largos took a slightly different approach to their Talk
Track. For one thing, they threw a catchy tagline in the front
of it. For another, the target audience is not specifically stated,
although it is definitely implied. We talked about it.

Loral's Coaching Clip

"You are starting off with a tagline," I said.

"Well, look," Dean said. "We're a pretty outgoing couple. And
everyone knows that I manage the grocery store."

"They're not really going to ask him his job," Anne said. "Or me
mine."

"What about when you meet people you don't know," I asked.

"I'm going to tell everyone about this new business," Anne said.
"We're going to kick off the conversation, and we wanted to say
something catchy."

"I think you are missing a chance for another distinction," I said.

"What's that?"

"You could say something about being personal and relationship-
oriented," I said. "Maybe you could be 'The Power Washing Couple.'"

"Yes," Dean said, "I like it."

———————

They sold me. I signed on the dotted line.

HELEN GREEN
Becoming Virtual

Helen was able to refine her ideas for her lemonade stand.

Helen's Five Key Distinctions

1. Experienced

2. Confidential

3. Resourceful

4. Willing to take on even small jobs

5. Calm, collected, nothing's a hassle

Distinctions need to be specific, but not necessarily unheard of. Though there may be other experienced virtual assistants in the market, Helen hoped her combination of experience and personality would be appealing.

She decided her Talk Track would be:

> "I'm a virtual assistant who can manage the billing and communication needs of any small-business owner with confidence, experience, and resourcefulness."

―――――

SEAN FITZPATRICK
Speeding Ahead

Confident, Sean believed he had many benefits to offer customers.

Sean's Five Key Distinctions

1. The tech comes right to your home or office.

2. No wait, immediate on-call service

3. Proprietary software that works effectively and efficiently

4. Experience

5. Reliability

Though he wasn't sure he could offer immediate service if he got too busy, Sean figured he'd be available in the beginning, and that that was a good distinct advantage at the start-up stage. Sean also balked at the third distinction, proprietary software. But he knew he was always going to use his own systems and procedures that would, eventually, become a software program.

While working on his Talk Track, Sean stumbled on the "to whom you provide the service or product" portion. After looking at the market of potential customers, Sean decided he needed another arena. He'd focus on individuals with computers, but the thought the bigger money might be found in commercial clients that didn't have an in-house tech department. And then, on a fluke, he decided to call the restaurant where he had recently tended bar. He asked the manager, who worked for his friend, how their computers were running. The answer was not positive. Sean wondered if he might be able to find a niche in small businesses and restaurants, through referrals.

In the meantime, he created his Talk Track:

> "You're in a hurry. Shouldn't your computer be, too? The Computer Cleanup Corps gets computers running fast and reliably for business owners and professionals who don't have time to waste."

Like the Largos, Sean used a tagline to prompt his Talk Track. He also included all the necessary parts: the name of the business, the service, its distinct advantage, and for whom the service was intended.

At this point, you too should be energized about your idea and excited to make more money. I'm hopeful you are eager to use your Talk Track, get out there, and *ask for the cash*.

EIGHT

ASK FOR THE CASH

When you ask for the cash, you will have a successful money-making venture. A money-making venture lives or dies by your ability to promote it. Asking for the cash is essential.

Asking for the cash does not mean you buy commercial time during the Super Bowl. Making more money fast is about getting the word out in the most cost-efficient and effective way possible. It may feel like a big step, but you've been doing it ever since you were little. Kids do it all the time. Think of the signs around lemonade stands. That's asking for the cash. The seller is trying to get you, the customer, to buy their product. That's asking for the cash.

To ask for the cash, you must:

- Have the papers ready.

- Define your customer.

- Find your customer.

- Craft the message that will explain your distinct advantages.

- Deliver the message to the customer.

But First: Your Brain

At this point, you've probably had to work on your language to redefine who you are and what you are trying to do; that is, adjust your identity. When it comes time to ask for the cash, you must adjust your brain. For some people, psychology and a difficult relationship with money get in the way of asking for the cash. Since you are moving at a quick pace to make $500 to $1,000 in the first month you are in business, your psychology needs to get up to speed with your need to ask for the cash immediately.

In this pursuit, it's helpful if you are confident. Again, that may seem easier said than done. But if you're not naturally confident, or you feel a bit fish-out-of-water trying to get your venture going, there's an age-old solution for you. Salesman have been doing it for years. It's called acting. Or more recently by other pundits, "fake it 'til you make it." If you act confident, you'll eventually be confident. I don't mean boastful or arrogant or cocky. Those are unappealing attitudes—and not confidence. Confidence is literally just belief in yourself. Act like you believe in yourself, and others will too. If you are already confident, hooray. Go get 'em.

When you ask for the cash, try this exercise. Put on the mask of your new self. The new self is the person who has come up with an idea, tested it, and is ready to launch it as a money-making venture. This will help you to get current with yourself. Have the person you are becoming do the asking. I'm not talking about becoming a professional house cleaner; I'm talking about becoming someone who's not worried about money, who knows they can make money, and who is sure that they are offering the customer an excellent opportunity in the form of a service or product.

Powerful language is always helpful. Sentences such as, "When do you want me to start?" and "How would you like to pay?" create an assumption that the deal is going to close.

Go back to the first Talk Track you came up with for you to introduce yourself. Now reframe it as a new Talk Track: a direct, positive pitch for business. For example: "I'm the owner of All-Natural Cleaners. I'd like to make your home healthy as well as spotless. I can schedule you for a day next week. Would Thursday work?" Write this new Talk Track down in the box on page 163. Commit it to memory. While it's a fine line between confident and aggressive, you can make your way to be effective with practice.

YOU SELL YOURSELF; THEN YOU SELL THE SERVICE.

The intention of this type of exercise is to get you clear on your intention. You are talking to people about your business with one goal in mind: to ask for the cash. Again, this should never be apologetic or reluctant. The customer is getting something they need, and you are providing that benefit to them.

Try to hold onto this psychology: Act with confidence. Believe in your product or service. Know that you are giving people what they want. Soon enough, your brain will know it, too.

ASK-FOR-THE-CASH TALK TRACK

Write down your direct, positive pitch for your money-making venture.

Have the papers ready.

It's not enough to just ask for the cash. You've got to be able to initiate, document, and seal the sale by getting a formal commitment down on paper. That requires four specific items.

1. The order form

2. A one-page contract

3. A flyer or other promotional material

4. Your price list

There can be anywhere from two to four pieces of paper for these, depending on your format. Some businesses have the contract on the back of the order form. Others put the price list right on the flyer. When you went through your Replicate and Duplicate step, you collected several examples from other companies. Use the ideas that work best for you.

People who are trying to make more money lose countless chances to do so for the simplest of reasons: They don't have an order form. They meet someone, pitch them, and then . . . hand over a business card and ask them to call. A lost opportunity to make money.

You want people to commit to buy sooner rather than later. If they do, they'll spend the time between their order and your delivery of the product or service looking forward to what they'll be getting. If they don't commit right away, they may spend the time between your pitch and their commitment having second thoughts. Or not thinking about it all. Get them to commit as soon as possible and they'll come up with the reasons to justify their purchase. If you don't get an immediate commitment, they'll come up with the reasons not to make the purchase and never call.

So you need a form on which you can record the contact information of the customer, what they're buying, when you're delivering it or providing it, and how they're paying for it. This doesn't need to be complex. You know how it's done. You've seen the Girl Scouts do it when they canvas your house for cookie sales.

Again, use your version of the order forms you discovered in your research. Other companies have already created great models so, again, don't reinvent the wheel. We also have some good examples on www.liveoutloud.com.

Define your customer.

Once you have the Ask-for-the-Cash Talk Track and an order form, you'll want to find your customers. Think about your lemonade stand in operation. See yourself working and collecting all that extra cash. Who's handing it to you? What do they look like? How would you describe them?

It's easy to think that everyone will want to hire you or buy from you. And eventually, everyone may. But for now, you've got to be very specific in describing your customers. Go back to the wisdom of the lemonade stand. That little table on your front lawn didn't draw people from the whole town. It targeted people who walked, biked, or drove down your street.

Start off by identifying those people who actually need, or have a use for, whatever it is you're selling. It is possible to convince people to buy things they didn't know they needed or wanted—consider the iPod—but it takes millions of dollars and a very compelling message. Your money and time should be devoted to targeting people who already want what you have to offer. Your goal will be to convince them to buy it from you.

Besides already needing your product or service, your customer also has to have enough money to buy it or hire you. People who are unemployed, for example, may need help developing and printing resumes. But targeting them as customers is not a great way to make money fast, since they don't have the extra money to spend. Focusing on people who can afford your offering is especially important for you since you're charging a premium price.

Once you have a picture of your customer in your mind, turn to page 167, titled "Potential Customers," and write down a description of them. (The rest of this form will be filled in as you go through the chapter.)

POTENTIAL CUSTOMERS

Write down a description of your customer.

Write down the names, addresses, and telephone numbers of the locations where you expect to find your customers.

Write down your message.

_____

Write down a brief description of the tools you'll use to deliver the message to your customers.

_____

Find your customer.

Your customers are people who need what you're offering and have the money to buy it. Now you have to find them; what is their geography?

The geographic limits you set on your market depend on the type of money-making venture you're starting. If you're starting a venture that relies on the Internet for your interaction with customers, your geography is the virtual world: people who have access to the Internet. If you're running a venture that requires you to physically visit multiple clients in a single day, you need to consider physical limits and decide what you are willing to do. You don't want to travel too far from your base of operations. Otherwise you won't be able to service many clients each day. However, if you're traveling to a single location where you'll be selling to multiple clients or customers, you shouldn't have a problem traveling a couple of hours or more each way for the chance to make a lot of sales.

In some cases it might be easy to find potential customers. Maybe they all work in the same kind of places; say, they're all public school teachers. You'd seek out the public schools in your area. Another example would be customers who all live in the same type of area. Perhaps you're selling something designed for people who live in apartments. Pinpoint multifamily dwellings in your geographic area and you've found potential customers.

Most times, however, it will be a bit more challenging. Instead of finding customers at their home or place of work, you might need to think about their lifestyle. What do all your potential customers share? What is it that they all do? Where is it that they all go?

Everyone, we hope, eats, so your potential customers probably go to the supermarket. But this may be too large and diverse a group. Dig even deeper into their lifestyle and try to come up with places only your customers go. The key is to put yourself into the life of your customer and visualize what they do during the course of the day.

For example, if your target customers are men in their twenties, you may find them at local sports bars, casual restaurants, hardware stores, sports shops, clothing stores, electronics stores, movie theaters, gaming arcades, parks, beaches, sports fields, courts, rinks, and gyms. You might also find them at special events, like concerts and sporting events.

Take out your local telephone directory or search the Internet, and look for the specific locations where you'll be able to find your customers. Turn back to page 167 and write down the names, addresses, and telephone numbers of all those locations. You're not going to target all these locations, but this is a helpful way to narrow in on the locations where it would be appropriate to approach your customer and where you can effectively deliver your message.

Craft the message and explain your distinct advantage.

You know whom you're after and where you'll find them. Next comes figuring out what to say to them: What's the right message to let them know that they want to buy what you're selling, from you?

There's no need to sell them on needing your product or service. The venture you've come up with was specifically created to meet an existing need. You already know you have customers who need what you are selling. That means your objective is to have them buy from you rather than someone else. Your message should deal with whatever it is that sets you apart from your competitors: your distinctions. If you've completed all the exercises we've gone through, this will be easy. Just go back to your original Talk Tracks and come up with a variation that you could see on a sign. Here's an example:

All-Natural Cleaners
A truly professional service for those who want
their home to be healthy as well as spotless.

Play around with different ideas. Run it past your community. Get their feedback and refine it further. When you have what you think is the right message, write it down on page 168.

Deliver the message to the customer.

The best message in the world is meaningless unless you can deliver it to your potential customers. There are many ways in which a product or service message can be delivered. We're going to look at three: advertising, promotion, and publicity.

It's important that all your advertising and promotional pieces not only convey the same general message, but share the same style and design. Develop one design and layout that works for flyers, posters, and your Web site, and a variation that works for your business cards, stationery, and car sign. This common design and layout will save you money and portray a professional image that helps your clients and potential clients remember who you are.

Most of the same applications that provide templates for flyers provide matching ones for business cards, letterhead, and invoices. Copy stores and print shops can insure that all your materials fit together well.

Rely on the Replicate and Duplicate method again. Look back at all the advertising and promotional materials you gathered when you were researching other businesses. See if there are elements you can adapt for your own business. Obviously, you wouldn't copy someone else's logo or graphics, but consider using the content as inspiration.

Advertising. Advertising is any type of ongoing effort to get your name and message in front of your potential clients and keep it there. Most likely television, radio, and print advertising are not within your budget. But advertising can still be an important part of your efforts. Instead of high-priced media, think about things like flyers, posters, business cards, refrigerator magnets, stationery, a sign for your car, a Web site, or a newsletter.

Flyers are a great tool for most lemonade stand ventures. You can hand out these single-sheet selling pieces, leave them in conspicuous places, or fold and send out as mailers. The same piece can serve all three purposes. Let's say you're targeting parents of young children for your all-natural cleaning service. You can ask an elementary school if you can hand out flyers in the lobby on the nights of concerts. You could ask the owners of hair and nail salons if you could leave a pile in their waiting area.

If you include your price list and an order form directly on your flyer, you'll have all you need to make more money. Rather than handing out business cards, you can introduce yourself with your Talk Track, show your flyer, ask for the cash, and fill in the order form. One piece of paper turns into fast cash. Take flyers and order forms with you wherever you go. Keep them in your car and in your purse, briefcase, or backpack.

What makes flyers even more fabulous is that they can be inexpensive to produce. If you have a good color printer at home you can design your own flyers. Some word processing applications come with built-in design templates that let you fill in the blanks and print out professional-looking materials. There are also some even higher-quality design templates available that you can use with your application. Do a quick Internet search and you're sure to find some. Once you do the design work, you can print out an original and have copies made, or print the copies yourself. If you don't have the right computer and printer at home, you can bring your ideas to a copy store; many will produce it for you.

Posters can be displayed in prominent places where your potential customers will see them. All-Natural Cleaners could put up posters on the bulletin board at the local supermarket, or by the checkout of the local health food store. As long as you get permission, place posters anywhere you think will be frequented by your potential customers.

For many lemonade stands, a Web site will be the virtual equivalent of a poster/order form. What matters most is that it delivers your message, conveys the same material as your flyers and posters, and provides an e-mail order form. It's worth it to get a domain name, because it sends a message that you're a serious business. Having a domain name is not costly. Take a look at the resources listed below.

Web Hosting

Here are some sources for inexpensive Web site hosting packages:

www.hostgator.com/
www.site5.com/
www.apollohosting.com/
www.hostnine.com/
smallbusiness.yahoo.com/webhosting/
www.godaddy.com/gdshop/hosting/
www.bluehost.com/

There are also lots of inexpensive ways to come up with a Web site design. Just don't let this slow you down too much . . . and maybe a local college or high school student can help. On page 175 you'll find a list of computer applications that let you design your site. You'll also find links to a number of online companies that will provide you with an inexpensive template or design services.

Do-It-Yourself Web Site Design

Here are some sites to explore applications that will let you design your own Web site:

Adobe Dreamweaver: tryit.adobe.com/us/cs4/dreamweaver/
   index.html
CoffeeCup Visual Site Designer: www.coffeecup.com/designer/
RapidWeaver 4.0: www.realmacsoftware.com/rapidweaver/
Apple iWeb: www.apple.com/ilife/iweb/

Online Web Site Design

Here are some online resources for designing your own Web sites:

order.1and1.com/
www.officeliveoffers.com/
www.site2you.com/
www.ixwebhosting.com/
www.websitewizard.com/

Online Networking

Develop your profile and post on social sites such as:

Twitter

Facebook

liveoutloudcommunity.com

MySpace

LinkedIn

Business cards are a good way to advertise. After you talk about your lemonade stand, you can hand out the business card. Leave a pile of cards at the offices of professionals who might recommend you. Consider turning the business card into a coupon entitling the bearer to a discount. Simply print the offer on the reverse of the card. Business cards can also become refrigerator magnets by putting sticky magnets on the back. These can be purchased at most office supply stores.

Sometimes, when I have a client who is working out their identity—that is, they can't quite fix it in their heads yet to be the new business owner—I suggest business cards as an aid. Consider making up a few different ones, each with a different identity. Try them out. Hand out one version at a party, see how it feels. It's an interesting exercise, and might grease the wheels for you to drive a bit quicker through any identity crisis.

Stationery isn't just a means of sending out invoices or letters. It can be a way to keep your name and message in front of customers every time you contact them. All-Natural Cleaners could leave a handwritten note on its stationery after each cleaning session. It needn't be anything poetic, it could just involve wishing the customer a happy upcoming holiday, or complimenting them on the new couch, or saying how much you love their home or appreciate their business.

You can use your stationery to send out a regular mailing, such as a newsletter, to your customers. This newsletter doesn't have to be a big deal. It could simply discuss changes in the business, such as new products or services you're offering, provide some helpful hints or tips, and solicit feedback, comments, or questions. Alternatively, you can send the newsletter out as an e-mail.

A magnetic sign for your car can be a smart investment. It won't be the most targeted advertising, but it's one more chance to get your name out there. If you live in the same area as your customers, or your full-time job is in the same town, a sign on your car can be an effective way to reach them. Call the nearest sign shop in your area, or check online for sizes and prices.

Promotions are one-time efforts to get your name out there. For a lemonade stand, this could include volunteer efforts, sponsorships, and special offers.

Volunteering your services for a local charity or cause could be a great way to get your message out while raising your business's profile in the community. Maybe All-Natural Cleaners could give the local chapter of the United Way a free cleaning session to offer as a reward for fundraising. Having the artistic director of the local theater company thank you before every performance of a play appealing to children, in exchange for your cleaning the theater after performances could be a great way to get your name in front of potential customers.

Special offers are another form of promotion that might make sense for a lemonade stand business. These could be mailers or e-mail messages suggesting products or services tied to upcoming calendar events. All-Natural Cleaners could send out a letter in early November offering special preholiday cleaning services for those hosting Thanksgiving, Christmas, and New Year's Eve gatherings, or special rates in the spring in honor of Earth Day.

Publicity is another way to deliver your message. This is unpaid coverage you receive from the media. While your lemonade stand may not be newsworthy on its own, you can try to get some media mentions by crafting press releases (on your stationery, of course) that could be helpful for journalists. Think of putting together a series of tips or suggestions and connecting them to some larger event. For example, All-Natural Cleaners could prepare a press release slated to run right after the holidays, offering tips on removing stains from tablecloths and carpets. There are many online resources to show you how to write press releases; many include free forms and samples. We also have some examples on www.liveoutloud.com.

Putting some or all of these ideas together will help you come up with a campaign to publicize your product or service. Use the ideas that make sense for your money-making operation. Now turn to page 168 on which you wrote your message. Underneath it, jot down your ideas for using advertising, promotion and publicity all together to deliver that message. This doesn't have to be formal. Just jot down what tools you're going to use, and where you'll be using them.

Collecting Rejection

There's something called the "10 percent rule" in sales: If you want five sales, you need to ask fifty people for the cash. Ten percent of those you ask will say yes. That can be a little daunting, but it can also be incredibly motivating if you think about it in pure numbers.

Let's say that you need two sales a month to generate $1,000 in new money a month. In order to get those two sales a month, you need to ask for the cash twenty times a month. Since we like to break things down into the 12/4/5, let's do that.

12: 20 times a month
4: 5 times a week
5: 1 time a day

In order to hit your $1,000 a month goal, you need to ask for the cash once a day. Simple. Straightforward. Doable. And stress-free. Since you need only two of those daily pitches to turn into sales each month, the pressure isn't that great.

If you're still unsure, don't worry, you're not alone. I've got an exercise to help you overcome your fears: Go out and ask for the cash until ten people say no.

That's right, I really want you to go get ten *rejections*. Use your flyer with the price list and order form and don't stop asking

until you get ten people to say no. Easy, right? After all, you're
expecting rejection.

As you will see, every "no" is a reason to celebrate, not get
depressed. Rejections aren't personal. And they contain lessons
for moving forward. Why did they say no? Take what you learn
from your first "no" and tinker with your new Ask-for-the-Cash
Talk Track so you can overcome the objection. Think about
whether you need to tweak your venture in any way.

REJECTIONS ARE OPPORTUNITIES.

Now go get another "no." Adjust your message based on what you
hear. Keep going until you have ten rejections. By the time you get
ten no's you may have one yes, so you'll have money coming in *and*
you'll have refined your Talk Track and your venture.

You've got to ask for the money over and over, every day.
That's the way to make more money.

***

MADELINE MATHEWS
Telling a Tutoring Tale

Madeline Mathews had never asked for money before, but she
was confident in her teaching skills. Drawing on her personality
she developed a new Talk Track to use as a sales pitch.

"I'm the teacher who can help your child reach his or her potential. When can we get started?"

She drew up a simple order form that could fit inside her appointment calendar, printed up a few dozen on her printer at

home, and started talking to her colleagues at work about potential clients.

Since she was going to be charging a premium for her one-on-one tutoring, Madeline knew she'd need to be smart about targeting her potential customers. She began with the most obvious group: parents of primary and secondary school students. Madeline narrowed this group further by income, believing that it was likely only parents who were middle class or above would be able to pay $100 an hour for tutoring. She then refined that group by drawing some geographic lines. She wanted to attract students who would be able to meet her at her school or at the library in town.

Madeline knew there were three large primary schools, two middle schools, and one very large high school that served kids who lived in her area. The mall in that part of town was a big draw for parents and kids alike. There was also a YMCA nearby that held lots of after-school activities.

There were lots of ways Madeline could reach her potential customers. Madeline had contacts at the other schools in her district. She decided she would approach the department chairs and guidance counselors at the schools, tell them what she was doing, and provide them with flyers. She'd ask the bookstore and toy store if she could put up posters. Madeline planned to approach the PTAs at the three schools she was specifically targeting and ask if she could either use their mailing lists or provide them with a flyer to include in their own mailings. She had created stationery that matched the rest of her materials, but she decided against using a sign for her car. She knew kids and parents might not want other people to know about the tutoring, so discretion outweighed any exposure the sign would bring.

Madeline also decided against flooding parking lots or anywhere else with flyers. She didn't think that would match the "elite" message she was trying to send. However, a special promotional mailing or e-mail a month or so before finals that offered special test prep sessions might make sense. Madeline wasn't sure if publicity would help her business since it might dilute the elite message. She decided she'd prepare a press release containing study tips and send it to the local newspapers at the same time she mailed out her test prep promotion and gauge the results.

Madeline reviewed her notes about her competitors, the things that would make her business unique, and her Talk Tracks. She put herself in the place of the parents she was targeting and thought about what would press their buttons. She came up with a message she thought would work:

One-on-One Tutoring
Have an award-winning teacher help your child reach
his or her potential . . . today and tomorrow

Loral's Coaching Clip

"You got it going on, Madeline. I like it. I especially like that you are talking to the principals and guidance counselors," I said. "And when are you going to get started?"

"Well, I'm still refining my poster," Madeline said. "My youngest daughter is coming up with some designs."

"Madeline, we want you to make money today," I said. "We want students coming to you immediately. What are you going to do right now to get a client?"

Madeline thought for a minute. She wasn't sure.

"Why are you delaying?" I asked, surprising her.

Then she realized. "I think I'm actually a little afraid to get my first client," she said. "The planning has been fine, but actually asking someone to pay me for what I've been doing for free for years? It feels strange."

"Of course it does," I said. "But it's not your fault that you gave away your value for so long. When you see how much more respect you get when you are paid to do what you are good at, you will be refueled and excited about your work. And that's a benefit to your students."

She nodded. She knew I was right. "I'm going to talk to my principal and some of the guidance counselors tomorrow. I'll see if they can refer any students to me and see if the guidance counselors will suggest to those parents that they call me. I'll also put an advertisement on the town's Web site tonight."

"Good," I said. "If you're lucky, you'll collect a no and learn from it."

_____

ANNE AND DEAN LARGO
A Fresh, New Look

Dean and Anne decided that their customers were homeowners who had vinyl siding that was getting a bit dirty and old. Finding the customer was going to be a local effort at first. Since the

Largos had determined that they wanted to create a relationship business and really know their customers, they hoped their customers would be neighbors and homes within a three-mile radius of their home.

In order to craft their message more effectively, they thought they should make some changes to their original Talk Track. Though they liked their catchy "Why paint when you can power wash?" slogan, they thought that it might confuse potential customers, since their homes would have siding, not paint. Working off the first Talk Track, they came up with an idea for their message.

Is Your House a Power House?
Recapture your home's original beauty with power washing.
It's inexpensive and efficient.
Call us today for an appointment,
Your friendly, reliable, neighborhood power (washing) couple,
Anne and Dean Largo

They hoped this would relay the benefits of the service they were providing, as well as their distinct advantage of being reliable and worthy of a relationship. They hoped too that the humor and personal touch would help capture the attention of potential clients.

In order to deliver the message, the Largos settled on several ideas, two of which they planned to initiate as soon as possible. The first was flyers. They would pay their kids to deliver the flyers to as many homes as they could within a two-mile radius. The second was e-mail. Their town had a Web site with a classified section. They would post their message under home maintenance. Moving forward, Dean hoped to ask some of his colleagues who managed the home improvement and hardware stores to post the flyers as well.

Anne also created business cards. On the back, she included a "Refer a Neighbor" 10 percent discount. She hoped that Dean, with the permission of his store's parent company, could hand these out at work, and she would hand them out whenever and wherever she could.

As a promotion and potential publicity event, Anne planned to ask the chamber of commerce if she and Dean could provide a free "Rain Shower" at this year's Run for Fun. The power washer had a gentle mist setting, and Anne thought it would create a perfect wall of water for runners in their last mile. Signs around them, as well as a pile of waterproof magnets to give away, would be a great way to promote their company.

HELEN GREEN
A Personal Message

Helen had never asked for money before and knew she needed help developing her Talk Track. At this point, she and I had decided her Talk Track was: "I'm a virtual assistant who can manage the billing and communication needs for any small-business owner."

She called a friend, who had a long successful career as an insurance agent, and spent an hour or so on the phone developing a pitch. They came up with a simple direct statement: "I can help a new business get started by setting up your online billing and creating any communication you need. I've done this type of work for thirty years and I'd like to start doing it for you this week. Would you like to meet next week? Perhaps, Monday?" Helen found a pad of standardized order forms at the office supply store and decided she'd use those until she got her own printed.

Her customers, she decided, would be owners of small businesses and start-ups. In order to find those customers, Helen planned to develop a relationship with several of the local banks and ask if they would consider referring her to new business owners. She knew most of these people would have a relationship with a bank, either to set up an account or get a small business loan. She also hoped to meet someone at the chamber of commerce who would introduce her to small-business owners. Simultaneously she thought she'd put up flyers in the local office supply stores.

The most difficult part of developing a Talk Track for Helen's lemonade stand was coming up with the right message. The problem wasn't in addressing the business owners; they would be eager to get good help. The issue would be any other staff. She knew from her experience in her husband's office that the staff might feel threatened by a freelancer. Helen realized that she needed to find business owners who had no staff like Kelly, the niece of her husband's former partner, who were really on their own and could use help with the tedious details of running a business.

Maximize Your Time, Leave the Details to Me
Wouldn't it be nice to have someone reliable and efficient:
set up your online banking and billing,
manage your billing to, and payments from, clients,
and handle the letter writing and phone calls for
which you don't have time?
Yes?
Then Helen Green is Your Gal (Monday through) Friday

Helen e-mailed Kelly with the message and asked her what she thought. Kelly liked it and agreed to e-mail it to some of her friends who were in a position similar to hers. Helen's hope was that she could rely on word of mouth alone. But she also knew that might not be enough.

She put her message on a one-page flyer, folded it to look more like a brochure, and included a list of the services she offered and a description of her experience working as office support staff. Helen decided not to include the price, hopeful that price might be an inquiry that would prompt a phone call. Confident of her personality, if not her business just yet, Helen felt she would do well on the phone with a potential client and wanted the opportunity for a conversation.

She planned to give the brochures to local banks and office supply stores. But rather than simply flooding them with the piece, Helen thought the best approach would be to personally visit each banker and store manager, speak with them, and get to know them. She knew this would be time consuming, but she believed that a face-to-face conversation would make a bigger impression than merely dumping brochures. She also knew that most of the time would be spent up front, and once she'd done well with the clients of the bank and customers of the office supply stores, that the bankers and store managers would think to refer to her on their own.

Helen also asked one of her granddaughters to create a Web site for her, where she hoped to post testimonials and references.

SEAN FITZPATRICK
Selling Speed

Sean quickly made a Web site for himself, with a tortoise and a hare right on the home page. He put a "You" T-shirt on the hare, and a "Your Computer" T-shirt on the turtle. Behind the turtle, he had squad of computer geeks ready and waiting with various fix-it tools. On the top of the page, he put his message, lifted from his Talk Track.

You're In A Hurry. Shouldn't Your Computer Be, Too?
Let the
Computer Cleanup Corps
get your computers running fast and reliably.
For business owners and professionals with no time to waste.

Satisfied with his Web site, which also included a page that bullet-pointed the reasons to have a computer checkup, Sean defined his customer. He determined that his customers were individuals who used their computers constantly and relied heavily on them for work or school. He thought he might be too pricey for college students, but he thought he'd test them out with flyers posted in and around the local schools, as well as postings on the Web sites he knew they visited. Sean also wanted to find individuals who worked on their computers all day and didn't have the support of an office computer tech. He put a posting on a freelancer Web site. Some of his freelancer friends also told him the key places they saw other freelancers working during the day, such as coffee shops, bookstores, and libraries. Sean posted flyers wherever he could. He also printed up several business cards to hand out when he was out at night or at the gym. He also planned to visit the coffee shops, bookstores, and libraries to hand out business cards and meet potential customers face-to-face.

Sean's other customer was the restaurant owner. He decided to spend one Saturday afternoon between the lunch and dinner hours, when he thought the restaurants would be slow, to do some meet-and-greet with the managers. He made flyers to leave behind, as well as his business card. With his friend's permission, Sean put his friend's name, restaurant, and phone number on the bottom of these flyers as a reference.

At this point, you are ready to roll. With one final check-through, it will be time to go, go, go . . .

NINE

THE BARE NECESSITIES

Some aspects of business are energizing. Some, less so. The good news is that even when you are doing paperwork, filling out forms, or adding up columns, it can be very exciting when the paperwork is a contract, the form is an order form, and those columns are profits. Every time I see a client make new money, week after week, month after month, they're glowing. It's just energizing. And no amount of paperwork can take that energy away from you now.

Now that you are ready to go and get things up and running, it's important to take a moment for a little reflection, just to make sure all the parts are in place and that there is a place for every part. Every business, even a lemonade stand, must have systems and procedures it follows. We are going to make sure you have yours.

As you move forward, you are going to want to:

- Create a checklist of the steps you need to take to get the lemonade stand up and running.

- Develop a procedure to follow from getting an order through to fulfilling that order.

- Track every dollar coming in and going out.

The right systems and procedures can make all the difference. If you can't track it, you can't control it. And now, with the right systems, the right software, the right rituals and procedure in your worklife, it's much easier to track your business. And you must track it, so you can control it. As I say, "you can do the paperwork, or you can be poor." It's an easy choice, right?

The Countdown Checklist

As every pilot knows, before you get in that airplane or helicopter you must, no matter how many times you fly, go over your preflight checklist. It's required. Even the most proficient pilots of all—the astronauts—do this. When NASA launches a space shuttle mission, its mission control center goes through a very detailed checklist to make sure every switch is set the right way and that every system is working properly. There's never 100 percent certainty that nothing will go wrong, but it is the best way to minimize the chance that there will be a problem. You've got to go through the same kind of countdown checklist before launching your lemonade stand.

Turn to page 194, titled "Countdown Checklist." You're going to write down every single thing you need to do before you formally start your money-making venture. Don't worry about putting them in any order. Just get everything down on paper. Include things you may have already done.

COUNTDOWN CHECKLIST

Here are some things to make sure you include: What office supplies do you require? What materials do you need? What equipment do you need to do your work? Do you have it all or are there some things you still need to buy? Write down what you already have, what you'll need to pack in your car or briefcase, as well as what you don't have and will need to buy.

Do you have a dedicated telephone line you'll be using for the business? If you don't, get a pay-as-you-go cell phone with voice mail, an inexpensive option for a business line. Arrange for the service provider to send you detailed bills so you can keep track of every call you make or receive.

Have you gotten a domain name for your Internet site? Having a site with your own name, rather than one through Google, Yahoo, or America Online, says you're a professional. Your e-mail address should be linked to whatever domain name you come up with.

Go back to the promotional plan. Have you designed and had your posters printed? Your flyers? Price list? What about your stationery and business cards?

Will you be using your car for the business? Get yourself a little auto record book while you're at an office supply store. This is just a little pad in which you can log the dates, times, and mileage of your business use while using your personal automobile.

Developing a Procedure for Orders

The next part of your paperwork is to create all the order forms, agreements, and contracts you'll need in the course of running the business. If you were able to gather forms from similar businesses while you were doing your research you've got a head start on this process. And even if you weren't able to obtain any of those other companies' forms, this won't be too daunting. In fact, it can be inspiring.

That's because the best way to figure out what forms you'll need is to visualize the whole process of getting and fulfilling orders. By doing this, you're going to picture how your business will succeed.

Let's start with your customers or clients. You've already come up with an order form, but now you'll also need either a sales agreement or a service contract. You don't need to hire a lawyer to come up with one of these. If you look on any form from a recent purchase, it usually has an agreement on it somewhere. And we have samples available at www.liveoutloud.com.

Read through whatever samples you have and alter them so they fit the specific nature of your business. This text from the contracts or agreements can become the proverbial fine print you put on your order form or flyer. If you do put the contract on your order form, have your customer initial this information when signing the order form.

What will you do with orders once you've taken them? You'll certainly need a file folder to put them all in, but you'll also need one place where you can record them all so you can prioritize them at a glance, perhaps by due date. How you do that depends on your style of working. It can be a simple paper form on which you list the job name and the rest of the important details, or it could be a whiteboard hanging over your desk. What matters isn't the exact type of the form; it's that you have one that in-cludes all your orders and that works for you.

Don't forget about collecting that money. When you finish the job, how will you bill your customer? Will you give them the bill personally and fill it in by hand? Or will you have an invoice you send by mail or by e-mail? For hand-written bills, you can find pads with carbons (so you can keep a copy) at office supply stores. If you'll be printing out your own invoices, look for a template that you can use with your existing stationery, or for a simple invoicing application. All you need to do is keep track of when you sent an invoice, and whether or not it has been paid.

Just a quick aside: a good replacement for accepting credit cards from customers is a PayPal account. It's easy to set up an account with which you can pay or accept payment from anyone with an e-mail address. Customers can set up a PayPal account for free and use their credit card to pay your invoices to them.

Tracking the Dollars

Besides your countdown checklist and your sales forms, the other paperwork system you'll need to set up is a bookkeeping system. The goal of your bookkeeping system is to have all the informa-tion you'll need to fill out your taxes.

There's no need for you to spend money on financial software right now. The applications are much more sophisticated than you need for your lemonade stand and will probably bring more confusion than clarity to your operation. All you need right now is some way of keeping track of how much money comes in, and from whom, and how much money goes out, and to where. That's easy to do with some simple accounting pads you can buy at office supply stores.

You'll need to track your spending on the categories of expenses used by the Internal Revenue Service on what's called a Schedule C. (See page 230 for a sample.) That's the form that tracks the profit or loss from a business run by a sole proprietorship, which is the one you'll use when it comes time to file your taxes.

This might include expenses such as:

- Advertising

- Car and truck expenses

- Commissions and fees

- Contract labor

- Depletion

- Depreciation

- Employee benefit programs

- Insurance (other than health)

- Interest (mortgage and other)*

---

*   Fear of losing access to health insurance is a key reason many people will not develop their own venture. They need insurance. Find health insurance choices at liveoutloudcommunity.com.

- Legal and professional services

- Office expenses

- Pension and profit-sharing plans

- Rent or lease (of vehicles, machinery, equipment, or other property)

- Repairs and maintenance

- Supplies

- Taxes and licenses

- Travel, meals, and entertainment

- Utilities

- Wages

- Other expenses

Your business probably won't have expenses in all these categories. And if you're going to be operating out of your home, you'll be deducting some of these expenses on Form 8829 for Business Use of Your Home. (See page 232 for a sample.)

Don't fall for all the stories about how claiming a home office can trigger an audit. The only time a home office is an audit risk is when the person claiming it has another place of business they're deducting as well. Since all you have for a place of business is your home, you're perfectly justified in claiming it as a deduction.

The way a home office deduction works is that you first measure the total interior square footage of your home. Then you measure the total square footage that you use for business. This includes not just your office area, but a path to an exterior door, as well as a bathroom and a path to that bathroom. Even the IRS lets you leave the office sometimes and use a bathroom. Let's say your entire home is 2,000 square feet and the area used for your business is 500 square feet. That means you can legitimately deduct 25 percent of some expenses on your home as home office deductions. The expenses you should track are:

- Mortgage interest

- Real estate taxes

- Insurance

- Rent

- Repairs and maintenance

- Utilities

- Other expenses

Let's see how our case studies would look at these tasks.

MADELINE MATHEWS
Teaching Benefits

Since Madeline Mathews was working full-time as a teacher, she had access to all the equipment she'd need for her tutoring business. Madeline had spoken with a close colleague who was a librarian in the district. He'd told her that she'd be able to get copies of all the textbooks she'd need through the school library system. She also knew she'd be able to get course outlines from other teachers. Besides text books and outlines, she'd just need pens and paper.

Rather than getting another line for her home, Madeline got a smartphone for the business. Since so many students today use text messaging and e-mail as their primary means of communication, she thought having ready access to those would make life easier for herself and her clients. The smartphone would also enable her to have constant access to her schedule and other information. She'd also be able to log her auto information on the smartphone.

Madeline asked her son to arrange for a Web domain and e-mail address for her. He created the Web site using her flyer. Madeline designed the flyer and the rest of her sales materials using templates that she downloaded for her word processing application. She was able to create the business cards and posters herself, but used a copy shop to run off multiple copies of the flyer.

Madeline took the service contract used by the subject tutoring business in town, simplified it, and altered it to fit her business. She also set up a simple spreadsheet program that she could use to record all her clients, and that she could edit on her smartphone. Madeline found a very basic invoicing program at the local computer shop that let her use the same template she'd created for her letterhead. She went online and opened a PayPal account in case any clients wanted to pay her with a credit card.

She also developed another simple spreadsheet to track her revenue and expenses. Among those would be some home office expenses, since Madeline decided to use part of her bedroom as an office.

ANNE AND DEAN LARGO
Power Paperwork

The idea for a power washing business came to the Largos specifically because they had the equipment. The water and electricity would come from the clients. Anne had a computer, and was proficient enough technically and with the design work to run their business from a home office. She would do the work in their den, at a desk they'd set up in the corner.

They decided to get a no-contract cell phone for the business. They also got their own domain name and Anne designed the site. They were going to use their digital camera to take before and after pictures and post them on the site.

Since Dean would use the car to transport the power washer, they would begin to track the mileage and gas usage.

The Largos also talked to their kids about getting involved. They were both eager. They'd take turns helping Dean out on the job, get paid, and he'd get that time with each of them.

Dean showed Anne how to use software he used at the supermarket. She then was able to create her own spreadsheets that duplicated the processes she'd learned on his software. She built the spreadsheets on the office software they had on their computer, and she was able to use it to keep track of each service, as well as record and build a history for each client.

Anne found a simple invoicing application online that she downloaded to their computer. Both Dean and Anne already had PayPal accounts and they agreed to use Dean's as a means for customers to pay with their credit cards.

Since Dean and Anne already used an online bookkeeping system for their personal finances and to prepare their taxes, they thought they'd simply use the same applications to track their business finances. Anne added expense categories to their current database that matched those they'd be filling in on a Schedule C. She also checked and discovered she'd be able to export that information to the tax preparation software they used. The same was true for a home office deduction. They'd simply measure the area that currently held their computer equipment and claim it as their business space.

———

HELEN GREEN
Keeping It Simple

Helen had all the equipment she needed: desk, a computer, printer, fax, and telephone. Since she rarely, if ever, used her cell phone, she decided to dedicate her cell phone to the business. She decided against the Web site, for now. She wanted to maintain only one

shingle for the moment, and that would be her home office, and
contact via e-mail and cell phone.

Though she was going to use her computer for communication
and billing for her clients, she'd keep track of her own business in
what she considered "good old reliable" notebooks. Using a filing
system from thirty years ago that made her comfortable, Helen
maintained one notebook for each client. She would also use her
filing system for order forms, agreements, and contracts.

As far as tracking her revenue, Helen had some experience
with an accounting software program. She knew she could
download that to her personal accountant for tax purposes.

Helen set herself up in the den, a room she rarely used anyway.
Now she'd dedicate that area to the business.

SEAN FITZPATRICK
Proprietary Plans

It crossed Sean's mind that he might need to invest either his
time developing, or his money acquiring, more sophisticated
virus scanning software. He knew that what he called the "real
pros" were using proprietary programs. At first, he would try to
use what he had. But eventually Sean hoped to build his own
virus scanning software. His bigger vision was to create something others would purchase.

Sean figured his biggest equipment needs were his software
and his scooter. He also decided to dress well and make an impression. The uniform of most computer-fix-it guys was sneakers,
jeans, and hooded sweatshirts. Though one company advertised

that their tech experts wore suits, he never saw that. Sean decided that would be his approach. He'd invest in a suit, a few shirts, and several gold ties, making that his color of distinction.

He wouldn't need much for his home office. Just the computer to check his Web site and e-mails. He'd use his current cell phone for now.

Sean found an order form he liked at a national electronics chain and copied it. Then he created a one-page contract. He also set up some spreadsheets to track his cash in and out. He'd always done his own taxes, but he decided that this year, he'd ask his older sister for the name of her accountant.

Home Work Tips

There's more to working from home than just calculating square footage and filling out tax forms. Basing your business at home offers financial advantages. Not only does it save you a major business expense—that is, office rent—but it actually helps you by turning a portion of money you're already spending on things like Internet and phone service into tax deductions.

Having a business in your home will affect you in other ways, too. Obviously, you'll be devoting some of the time you now spend on your personal life to business issues. And you might be surprised to discover how the time you devote to business has a tendency to grow. When you work at home there's very little separation between personal and business life. The office is always there. The telephone is always there, ringing while you're eating dinner. The computer is always there, tempting you to check your e-mail when you could otherwise be playing with the kids or chatting with your spouse.

For the health of your emotional life and relationships, you're going to need to set some boundaries. These don't need to be etched in stone. When projects are pressing you'll want the freedom to work later and just have pizza for dinner. Still, you need to make sure you don't strain your family or marriage while building a business. Pay attention to this potential problem, and create rules for yourself to follow that will protect your family, yourself, and your business.

Another issue you're likely to face is that friends and family don't think you're really working because you're at home. They'll call you when you're in your home office much more freely than they'd call you at an outside office. They may just stop by when you're working, expecting you'll be able to spend time with them. Explain to them that you are working when you're in your home office and will give them your undivided attention when you can.

Action is your best friend.

Now it's time to execute. You're ready. You've read up to this page, filled in the charts, and gotten your materials together. You can be off to ask for the cash in a matter of days.

You will learn more in one hour of execution than you could ever learn reading, thinking, or planning. Once you're out there in action, running your lemonade stand, you will get an immediate feel for what's working and what's not. Imagine the charge of excitement when you make your first sale. Well, you don't need to, it's there for the taking.

TEN

OPENING DAY AND BEYOND

Congratulations. Look at you. You're here. Ready to put that lemonade stand out on the lawn.

You've:

- uncovered your skills and resources,

- come up with an idea, and

- examined its money-making potential.

You've:

- researched similar businesses,

- modeled their best practices, and

- created your distinct advantage.

You've:

- studied comparable prices,

- settled on a premium price,

- written a Talk Track, and

- fleshed out your business idea.

You've:

- defined your customers,

- located your customers,

- crafted a compelling, distinct message, and

- decided on the best ways to deliver that message.

You've:

- begun your paperwork,

- put together an order form,

- collected sample agreements and contracts, and

- laid the groundwork for systems to track dollars in and out.

And now here you are, ready to launch your lemonade stand.

The first day of any new venture is exciting. And it can be a little nerve-wracking. Which, as you know, is like anything new. And as with anything new, when you finally get through that first day, or in this case, first few hours, a lot of the concern goes away. But jumping past those fears and just moving forward, is not always easy. I know. I feel that same fear every time I start anything new, even now. Because I always get through each start and feel good once I'm in action, I know you will, too.

If you have negative thoughts, find some little box in your brain and lock them away in there. I can even guess what they are. Please allow me to stomp on them, and provide you with the positive thoughts on which you can rely:

- You will succeed.

- You've done enough right, and considered what you need to consider.

- You have enough time to run this lemonade stand.

- Customers will want to pay you for what you are offering.

- You will be paid what you are asking.

- You are cut out to run a lemonade stand.

- You are ready.

- This will succeed.

Positive thoughts are necessary to succeed. And the fastest road to positive thinking is positive action. That's right, the action comes first. Get out there and start your business. Then you will have the experience that proves you are capable. That evidence will reinforce your confidence. That confidence will get you out there again.

ACTION → EXPERIENCE → EVIDENCE
→ CONFIDENCE → ACTION

Will you have some bad days? Sure. But in business, bad days are something to be proud of, because it means you are out there doing it. Even if you stumble along during the first few days of your lemonade stand, soon enough you'll see a hint of progress. The next thing you know, that hint will become a definite sign and you will be moving forward, fast.

As soon as you can, make a call or put up a flyer, or put up a post on a Web site, to announce your lemonade stand. Make it your goal, in the next three days, to get your first customer.

Once you begin your venture, and the money starts to come in, you'll see how exciting it can be. After you work out the kinks, you'll be reeling in $500 to $1,000 a month in extra cash. You may even find, as have many of my clients, that it doesn't take much more effort to bring your operation to the next level. When things start zooming along, you'll want to have the foundation ready to support a bigger venture.

Formalize the business.

One of the secrets to getting cash in your pocket fast is to approach your lemonade stand in as simple and informal a manner as possible. Once you're up and running, the money will be coming in. But to keep that cash flowing and to increase it, you need to start formalizing what you've already done.

Contact City Hall. Visit your city, town, or village hall. Head for the clerk's office and explain that you're starting a business and want to know what kind of licenses and forms you need to file. The rules and fees vary by state, city and county. (See the chart on page 212 for some examples.) You'll probably need to obtain a business license, although some municipalities waive that requirement if you're operating from your home. This will cost a nominal fee. If you're doing business under a name different than your own, you'll also have to file a DBA form. That stands for "doing business as," and is also called a "fictitious business statement." The purpose of this is to let the public know who's actually operating the company.

Selected Business License Requirements and Fees

Atlanta, Georgia: All businesses are required to have a business tax certificate and license. Fees are based on income level and, if over $10,000 per year, on type of activity. For businesses generating an income of under $10,000, there's a one-time fee of $50 and a $75 annual registration fee. There's also a $15 annual surcharge per employee.

Boston, Massachusetts: All businesses need a license, which must be renewed every four years. The fee is $50.

Chicago, Illinois: All businesses need a license. The fee depends on the business activity, but home-based businesses are assessed $250.

Dallas, Texas: All businesses need a license. The fees are based on the location of the business. Home businesses are exempt but must have a state tax ID and must file a DBA statement.

Las Vegas, Nevada: All businesses need a license. The fees are based on the business activity and are determined through a discussion with local staff.

Los Angeles, California: All businesses need a license, but you are exempt from paying a fee if it earns less than $100,000.

Los Angeles County, California: The requirement for a license depends on what type of business you're operating. The fees range from free to $2,254.

Miami, Florida: All businesses need a license. Fees depend on the location of the business and the type of activity. The fee for a home office is approximately $100.

Phoenix, Arizona: All businesses need a tax license. The total fees are based on the business activity, but the standard application fee is $20.

San Diego, California: All businesses need a license. The fees are based on the number of employees. If you have twelve or fewer, it costs $76.

San Jose, California: If the annual income for the business is above the poverty line, which changes each year, a license is necessary. It costs $35.

Talk to a lawyer. Next you'll want to contact a lawyer and have him or her look over your sales agreement or service contract. Since you're already starting off with a document, rather than having one drawn up from scratch, this will probably only take an hour or two of the lawyer's time. That means it will cost you anywhere from $100 to $200, depending where you're located. Explain to the lawyer that you'll be coming back in the near future to discuss incorporating your business. The potential for future fees from you should insure he or she keeps the bill to a minimum.

Get an EIN. Contact the Internal Revenue Service either by telephone or online (www.irs.gov) and ask for an EIN (Employer Identification Number). There's no charge to obtain this number. An EIN is a requirement for businesses which have employees, but it also makes sense for solo operators like you. Even though your personal Social Security number could serve the same purpose, it looks more professional and is probably safer to use an EIN instead. You should also look into the requirements in your state; you can do this on your state's Web site. (Try entering the state's name with the ending dot-gov, for example, www.nevada.gov.)

Open a bank account. Go to your local bank, preferably the one where you have your personal accounts, and explain that you've started a money-making venture and would like to open another bank account. Unless you've got a lot of money already on deposit with the bank, odds are they aren't going to provide you with a lot of merchant services, like the ability to accept MasterCard or Visa. However, make sure you at least get an account that lets you write unlimited checks, pays some kind of interest on your balance, and provides access through an ATM/debit or credit card. While you're at the bank, arrange for online banking access to this new account, and your personal accounts, if you're not already able to access them online. Find out what personal finance software works best with the bank's online system.

Computerize your bookkeeping. It's time to graduate to a computer-based bookkeeping system. Quicken and QuickBooks are the most popular applications, but they may be more sophisticated that you need. There are many other choices which will do the job just as well. Some are easier. Most will let you download a demo copy and try it for a short period of time before purchasing a license. Look for an application that will work for both your business and personal needs, that you can integrate with online banking, and that will let you print out checks.

Join the business community. It's also time for you to join the business community. Contact your local chamber of commerce and see what services they offer and what programs they run. Rather than joining as a business, see if you can join as an individual; the cost will be dramatically different. Reach out to the local Rotary Club and take in a meeting. Affiliating with these groups will help reinforce your new self-image as a business owner. They can also provide great networking opportunities.

However, the rewards you receive from joining these kinds of organizations are directly related to the extent of your involvement. Our entrepreneurial community is liveoutloudcommunity.com, where thousands of people making money have daily conversations and share résumés. It's those who are regularly involved who will receive the most referrals and get the most open response to questions and requests for help and advice.

Expand your operations. There's no such thing as a static business. All businesses, even lemonade stands, are either growing or dying. That's because the world is always changing. Your customers' needs are different this year from last year and will be different again next year. Your market is a moving target, and unless you keep adjusting your aim you'll lose sight of it and start losing business as a result. But there are different ways to grow, some of which will let you maintain the simple nature of your lemonade stand.

Widen your market. The most obvious way to grow is to seek out additional customers, widening the market you're targeting. The advantage of this approach is that it offers the opportunity to make the most money in the long run. More clients can mean more revenue. And the good news is that in some businesses, more customers does not necessarily mean more time. It depends how volume sensitive your business is. For example, if you are making and selling T-shirts at weekend crafts fairs, you hope to attract more customers. You're there anyway, your time is already spent. But if you are a service business and you deal with each client one-on-one, then more customers usually translates to a need for more time. A solution there, of course, is to hire more people to work with you and service the customers. If you don't want to hire more people, you can get help through commissions and referrals. There are many ways to deal with an increase in customers without sacrificing too much of your time.

Commissions and referrals. More hands mean more work gets done. But if you feel employees are too expensive and require too much management, or that a partner is unappealing because you don't want to share ownership or decision making, you can consider some kind of commission or referral arrangement. There are many ways to do this. For example, you might offer someone a flat rate or percentage of sales commission for every new customer cultivated and serviced. Or you could expand and formalize referral arrangements in which you and a complementary business pass potential clients back and forth in exchange for a finders fee or commission.

Create more products or services. Another way to grow your lemonade stand or pushcart business is to develop additional products and services that would be of interest to your existing market. Customers appreciate the convenience of one-stop shopping. If they're already enrolled as your customer and have a relationship with you, they know you are reliable and offer quality. A house-cleaning business, for instance, could expand into closet organizing or auto detailing. A lawn care business could expand into snow shoveling or houseplant care. A catering business could offer its clients a grocery shopping service. The idea is to think about the other needs your existing customers have, and come up with solutions that you are logically able to provide and that they would be happy to purchase from you.

MADELINE MATHEWS
Targeted Teaching

For four months after launching her tutoring business, Madeline Mathews was pulling in $1,000 a month. During the summer months, however, her earnings dropped to below $500, and that gave her some time to think about where she could take the business.

Madeline felt confident that she would be able to continue earning $1,000 a month during the school year but was concerned that during the summer her income wouldn't keep up. She thought she wouldn't have the time to do much more tutoring during the school year, so she couldn't take on more clients to make up for the lack of business during the summer. Madeline was already charging a premium and was afraid increasing her prices would alienate her existing clients. She then thought about the fact that many of her high school clients would be taking the PSAT and SAT exams. Though there already existed prep classes for those standardized exams, and a few tutors as well, Madeline believed she'd be able to offer short-term, small-group, targeted tutoring, to her existing clients.

ANNE AND DEAN LARGO
Powering Forward

The Largos' business took a few months to get going. They had the idea in the winter and knew their customers wouldn't be interested in power washing until the spring. But they used those winter months to lay the groundwork and spread the word, and during the spring the business took off. By July they were pulling in $1,500 a month, and their time was well managed. Dean took five hours to clean a large home, and did one a week. Some clients asked him to do the driveway or a fence as well. Anne spent about six hours a week managing and promoting the company.

By the end of the summer, the Largos decided they wanted to expand the business. Their wall shower publicity stunt at the Run for Fun got their picture in the paper, as well as a few new customers. But at this point, most of their customers came from the area that they had showered with flyers, which was the neighborhoods within a two-mile radius of their home. They decided to push the promotion a bit by posting their service on more Web sites and putting up more flyers in town.

Loral's Coaching Clip

"How about some more services?" I suggested.

"We're already doing driveways and fences," Dean said. "That increases our revenue, but it also extends the amount of time I spend at each home."

"I always tell clients that it's best to sell to the many through the one," I said. "If you can pitch in one place, and get a lot of people through that, it's very efficient. In this case, your issue is time efficiency. We need to find that one place where you can do a lot more business per visit without investing a lot more time. Perhaps a commercial customer, instead of residential. Someone who has a lot of things to wash, but none of which take too much time."

"We can't do the auto dealerships, they clean their cars with much more care than I can offer through a power washer," Dean said. "Even the used car lots wouldn't want my service."

"And I tried four marinas," Anne said. "They all have someone they already use."

"Farm equipment?" I asked.

"The dealers clean their own equipment," Dean said.

"Did you try the strip malls?" I asked.

"They have someone under contract," Anne said.

It was clear the Largos had a lot of energy and ideas. They'd really made the effort to find a different type of customer. I was impressed. Even though they weren't breaking into a new business avenue yet, Anne and Dean had the drive to collect the no's. They were on their way to becoming successful business owners.

I thought about the more-things-to-wash angle for a moment. "Do you know the superintendent of schools?" I asked.

"I'm pretty sure they have someone on the town contract," Anne said.

"Do they do the playgrounds, and the Dumpsters, and the little things that no one thinks about, like the garbage cans?" I asked.

Anne and Dean shared a look, a look that brightened. "I don't think they do those things," Anne said. "How would we charge for that?"

"Give him an overall rate, for all of the schools in town," I said. "Then figure out how many hours it will take to do the power washing at each school, figure out how many hours you want to work a week, and how many schools there are, and give him a number."

She jumped on the phone and left a message for the superintendent. She hoped she and Dean could impress the superintendent with their personal appeal and get him to consider them for cleaning the playgrounds, Dumpsters, garbage cans, and maybe even the outdoor basketball courts at the schools.

"I think I'll call the town's parks and recreation department, too," Anne said, dialing. "Dean, honey, you could become the King of Clean Garbage Cans." She smiled, enthusiastically. He nodded, a little less enthusiastic.

They were energized to make more money. By the end of the year, I was pretty sure, they'd double their revenue.

HELEN GREEN
A Personal Push

Not quite comfortable yet selling herself during her phone calls with business owners, Helen Green was already working more hours a week than she projected. She only wanted to work five hours a week, at $25 an hour, to make $125 a week and $500 extra new money a month. But Kelly, her first client, was impressed with the followup letters to her clients that Helen was writing for her. Kelly said that her clients commented on the personal touch, and how nice it made them feel. Kelly told another business friend about Helen, and soon Helen was working ten hours a week and making $1,000 a month.

Six months later, Helen was still earning $1,000 a month, and enjoyed her two clients. But Kelly's business started to grow, and she needed more in-house, not virtual, staff. Kelly tried to help Helen find another client, but she was very busy now with her business. She told Helen she'd be a reference. Though Helen wasn't interested in growing her business too much, she was quite enjoying that extra $1,000 a month.

As a virtual personal assistant, Helen knew that the communications part of her work was her best. She tried to think of someone who could use a good letter writer. A few days later, she was looking through her mail, and found a much delayed letter from her local congressman. He was responding to her frustration with the lack of parking at the public beaches. His letter was formal and impersonal. Helen then recalled that years ago, her daughter worked in Washington, D.C., as what they called a legislative correspondent. Her daughter wrote personal letters to constituents. Obviously, the local congressman had no such person. Having hit on another skill set, Helen decided to expand her market of potential customers. She wrote a letter of proposal to the congressman.

He didn't hire her. His budget didn't allow for it. But he liked her letter and responded personally. After they spoke, he then referred her to another business in town that did hire her. And a year later, Helen had five clients who needed a virtual assistant for their communications.

Rarely have I seen a good effort go unrewarded. Though Helen's idea to work for the congressman was not the right idea, her effort to test the idea led to an unexpected but fruitful result. Specific and targeted efforts may not always pay off the way we think they are going to. But in some way, they are usually worth the effort.

———

SEAN FITZPATRICK
Positioning His Own Product

Sean was doing very well with his lemonade stand. Not only were several individuals hiring him to speed up and clean up their computers, but the commercial side of his business was thriving. He was on retainer, for a monthly fee, to six different restaurants in town and two large restaurant chains.

Committed to pursuing his dream of creating a technology start-up, Sean spent several hours each week building a new virus scan-search-eradicate software application. He was able to test it with his customers. Sean soon learned that few companies sold this type of application to individuals. They'd rather make the money through their viral cleanup services. Sean decided he'd turn that process around. His goal was to put himself out of business by selling the eradication software directly to his customers. He hoped his lemonade stand would become his tech start-up.

As you can see, once you get started, there are many ways to expand and grow your business. The key is to get started.

ELEVEN

BREAK THE PATTERN

When you start your lemonade stand, you will see that making new money is easier than you ever thought possible. But your accomplishment is much bigger than you think it is. There is more to it than $1,000 of new money every month. There's more to it than a little independence and a lot of empowerment. There's more to it than the potential to turn that $1,000 into $10,000 a month, or more. Your accomplishment is significant because you've broken the pattern. A pattern of spending, saving, spending, and saving that's crippled the capacity of too many for too long. The new pattern is to make money and use that money to live the way you want to live, build a stable financial future, and perhaps, if you're driven, to create wealth.

In order to break that pattern, you accomplished a very significant task. You were able to:

LEARN TO EARN.

It sounds simple. It may appear obvious. But the truth is, in all our years of education we never really learn to earn. We learn *about* earning, we may even get a vocational class here and there, but we never learn specifically *how* to turn what we know into dough, so to speak. This is what the lemonade stand is about. It's about finding a way to make money, today. There's not a lot of philosophy or discussion. It's about doing, it's about action.

One of the reasons this accomplishment of yours is significant is because now you have the opportunity to break the pattern by passing on this new legacy to your children, or the kids in your life, or the next generation in general. This is your chance to pass on an amazing legacy by saying, "Here's how to make your life a whole lot easier."

The only way to break the repeating generational pattern of money misinformation is to teach young people what we weren't taught. We need to encourage a new generation of lemonade stand ventures and coach them to strive to believe in abundance, not in scarcity.

You are, of course, a model for your children. And now you can take them into the new world you've created with your money-making venture. You don't have to sit them down for a birds-and-the-business kind of talk. You can teach them about what you are doing by including them in what you're doing.

There are many ways to include kids in your lemonade stand. Ways that will engage and enroll them, such as:

a. Ask your children what they think your skills are. Their answers may surprise you and open up some more areas for you to consider.

b. Ask your children what resources you have available to you to help support you in a business. Maybe they'll even offer up themselves and their skills.

c. Get your children's ideas on lemonade stands that would use your skills and resources.

d. Have them help you ask for the cash. Children are great salespeople!

Asking the advice of children is beneficial in many ways. For one, it opens up your mind to new ideas. Two, it enrolls them. Children like to be experts, sought after for their thoughts. Unfortunately, that is too rarely done. Three, it's a nice way to open up conversation and share time together.

These discussions about your lemonade stand will help you to promote a healthy relationship with money for you and your children. Never again will you say "We can't afford that." Instead, you will instill in them a desire to make the money they need to afford whatever they want. Encouraging kids to live out loud about money removes the stigma and taboo, and allows children the freedom to approach making money as just one aspect of living life well.

Another great way to break the pattern and help your children learn to earn is to help them set up their own lemonade stand. Work with them to uncover their skills and resources. I know from my conversations with my son that this exercise can be quite thrilling for a parent. There's little that's more exciting than hearing your child share and affirm his or her abilities. Help your child come up with an idea that uses those skills. Many kids, always creative, won't need a lot of help, just a little guidance, maybe some steering in a productive and simple direction. The key is to keep your child interested. And this means keeping things productive and simple.

Price out their business so your child can see if the effort is worthwhile. If it's not, help them come up with—and quickly work through—another idea, so they learn not to hold too dear just one concept.

As they move forward, help them with their promotion materials and spreading the word. It's essential that you manage this process, and it's your responsibility to oversee it. The last thing you want is a bunch of customers showing up at your front door for a product your child advertised over the Internet.

Provide your child with systems to track their sales. Talk about the pattern of money and where their income should go, including taxes, if applicable, charities, and good works, and their own personal investment. Consider opening a bank account for them and helping your child learn about the power of compound interest over time.

As you know, most schools aren't geared to do this, yet. It's up to you and me. (I've actually set up an online program for just this purpose at loralskids.com.) We need to do our best to eradicate financial illiteracy in this next generation. Teach the children the realities rather than the myths about money. Share with them the possibility of abundance. Show them that they are worthwhile and should pursue a bigger life. Be direct; stay affirming and positive. Ask them open-ended questions so you can engage in dialogue. Help them form the lifelong patterns that will lead to a life of prosperity and a healthy attitude toward money. Live out loud with them each and every day. And work with them to launch their own lemonade stands, whatever their age. Teach them what you've just learned, the secret to living a fuller life, the way to escape the old patterns. Show them how they can put more money in their pocket.

Here's to a new pattern. A pattern of abundance, and living well.

APPENDIX

Here are some sample forms that might be useful to you. Check the IRS web site for the most up-to-date versions.

SCHEDULE C
(Form 1040)

Department of the Treasury
Internal Revenue Service (99)

OMB No. 1545-0074

2008

Attachment
Sequence No. 09

Profit or Loss From Business
(Sole Proprietorship)
▶ Partnerships, joint ventures, etc., generally must file Form 1065 or 1065-B.
▶ Attach to Form 1040, 1040NR, or 1041. ▶ See Instructions for Schedule C (Form 1040).

Name of proprietor	Social security number (SSN)

A Principal business or profession, including product or service (see page C-3 of the instructions)	B Enter code from pages C-9, 10, & 11 ▶

C Business name. If no separate business name, leave blank.	D Employer ID number (EIN), if any

E Business address (including suite or room no.) ▶
City, town or post office, state, and ZIP code

F Accounting method: (1) ☐ Cash (2) ☐ Accrual (3) ☐ Other (specify) ▶

G Did you "materially participate" in the operation of this business during 2008? If "No," see page C-4 for limit on losses ☐ Yes ☐ No

H If you started or acquired this business during 2008, check here ▶ ☐

Part I Income

1	Gross receipts or sales. **Caution.** See page C-4 and check the box if: • This income was reported to you on Form W-2 and the "Statutory employee" box on that form was checked, or • You are a member of a qualified joint venture reporting only rental real estate income not subject to self-employment tax. Also see page C-4 for limit on losses. ▶ ☐	1
2	Returns and allowances	2
3	Subtract line 2 from line 1	3
4	Cost of goods sold (from line 42 on page 2)	4
5	Gross profit. Subtract line 4 from line 3.	5
6	Other income, including federal and state gasoline or fuel tax credit or refund (see page C-4)	6
7	Gross income. Add lines 5 and 6 ▶	7

Part II Expenses. Enter expenses for business use of your home only on line 30.

8	Advertising	8		18 Office expense	18
9	Car and truck expenses (see page C-5)	9		19 Pension and profit-sharing plans	19
10	Commissions and fees	10		20 Rent or lease (see page C-6):	
11	Contract labor (see page C-5)	11		a Vehicles, machinery, and equipment	20a
12	Depletion	12		b Other business property	20b
13	Depreciation and section 179 expense deduction (not included in Part III) (see page C-6)	13		21 Repairs and maintenance	21
				22 Supplies (not included in Part III)	22
14	Employee benefit programs (other than on line 19)	14		23 Taxes and licenses	23
				24 Travel, meals, and entertainment:	
15	Insurance (other than health)	15		a Travel	24a
16	Interest:			b Deductible meals and entertainment (see page C-7)	24b
a	Mortgage (paid to banks, etc.)	16a		25 Utilities	25
b	Other	16b		26 Wages (less employment credits)	26
17	Legal and professional services	17		27 Other expenses (from line 48 on page 2)	27

28	Total expenses before expenses for business use of home. Add lines 8 through 27 ▶	28
29	Tentative profit or (loss). Subtract line 28 from line 7	29
30	Expenses for business use of your home. Attach Form 8829	30
31	**Net profit or (loss).** Subtract line 30 from line 29. • If a profit, enter on both **Form 1040, line 12,** and **Schedule SE, line 2,** or on **Form 1040NR, line 13** (if you checked the box on line 1, see page C-7). Estates and trusts, enter on **Form 1041, line 3.** • If a loss, you **must** go to line 32.	31
32	If you have a loss, check the box that describes your investment in this activity (see page C-8). • If you checked 32a, enter the loss on both **Form 1040, line 12,** and **Schedule SE, line 2,** or on **Form 1040NR, line 13** (if you checked the box on line 1, see the line 31 instructions on page C-7). Estates and trusts, enter on **Form 1041, line 3.** • If you checked 32b, you **must** attach **Form 6198.** Your loss may be limited.	32a ☐ All investment is at risk. 32b ☐ Some investment is not at risk.

For Paperwork Reduction Act Notice, see page C-9 of the instructions.   Cat. No. 11334P   Schedule C (Form 1040) 2008

Part III   Cost of Goods Sold (see page C-8)

33 Method(s) used to
value closing inventory: a ☐ Cost   b ☐ Lower of cost or market   c ☐ Other (attach explanation)

34 Was there any change in determining quantities, costs, or valuations between opening and closing inventory?
If "Yes," attach explanation . . . . ☐ Yes   ☐ No

35 Inventory at beginning of year. If different from last year's closing inventory, attach explanation . .	**35**	
36 Purchases less cost of items withdrawn for personal use	**36**	
37 Cost of labor. Do not include any amounts paid to yourself	**37**	
38 Materials and supplies	**38**	
39 Other costs	**39**	
40 Add lines 05 through 30	**40**	
41 Inventory at end of year	**41**	
42 **Cost of goods sold.** Subtract line 41 from line 40. Enter the result here and on page 1, line 4 . .	**42**	

Part IV   Information on Your Vehicle. Complete this part **only** if you are claiming car or truck expenses on line 9 and are not required to file Form 4562 for this business. See the instructions for line 13 on page C-5 to find out if you must file Form 4562.

43 When did you place your vehicle in service for business purposes? (month, day, year) ▶ _____ / _____ / _____

44 Of the total number of miles you drove your vehicle during 2008, enter the number of miles you used your vehicle for:

a Business _____ b Commuting (see instructions) _____ c Other _____

45 Was your vehicle available for personal use during off-duty hours? . . . . ☐ Yes   ☐ No

46 Do you (or your spouse) have another vehicle available for personal use? . . . . ☐ Yes   ☐ No

47a Do you have evidence to support your deduction? . . . . ☐ Yes   ☐ No

b If "Yes," is the evidence written? . . . . ☐ Yes   ☐ No

Part V   Other Expenses. List below business expenses not included on lines 8–26 or line 30.

--		
--		
--		
--		
--		
--		
--		
--		
48 Total other expenses. Enter here and on page 1, line 27	**48**	

Form **8829**	**Expenses for Business Use of Your Home**	OMB No. 1545-0074
	▶ File only with Schedule C (Form 1040). Use a separate Form 8829 for each home you used for business during the year.	**2008**
Department of the Treasury Internal Revenue Service (99)	▶ See separate instructions.	Attachment Sequence No. **66**

Name(s) of proprietor(s)	Your social security number

Part I Part of Your Home Used for Business

1	Area used regularly and exclusively for business, regularly for daycare, or for storage of inventory or product samples (see instructions)	1	
2	Total area of home	2	
3	Divide line 1 by line 2. Enter the result as a percentage	3	%

For daycare facilities not used exclusively for business, go to line 4. All others go to line 7.

4	Multiply days used for daycare during year by hours used per day	4	hr.	
5	Total hours available for use during the year (366 days × 24 hours) (see instructions)	5	8,784 hr.	
6	Divide line 4 by line 5. Enter the result as a decimal amount	6		
7	Business percentage. For daycare facilities not used exclusively for business, multiply line 6 by line 3 (enter the result as a percentage). All others, enter the amount from line 3 ▶	7		%

Part II Figure Your Allowable Deduction

8	Enter the amount from Schedule C, line 29, **plus** any net gain or (loss) derived from the business use of your home and shown on Schedule D or Form 4797. If more than one place of business, see instructions	8	

See instructions for columns (a) and (b) before completing lines 9-21.

			(a) Direct expenses	**(b) Indirect expenses**	
9	Casualty losses (see instructions)	9			
10	Deductible mortgage interest (see instructions)	10			
11	Real estate taxes (see instructions)	11			
12	Add lines 9, 10, and 11	12			
13	Multiply line 12, column (b) by line 7	13			
14	Add line 12, column (a) and line 13				14
15	Subtract line 14 from line 8. If zero or less, enter -0-				15
16	Excess mortgage interest (see instructions)	16			
17	Insurance	17			
18	Rent	18			
19	Repairs and maintenance	19			
20	Utilities	20			
21	Other expenses (see instructions)	21			
22	Add lines 16 through 21	22			
23	Multiply line 22, column (b) by line 7		23		
24	Carryover of operating expenses from 2007 Form 8829, line 42		24		
25	Add line 22 column (a), line 23, and line 24				25
26	Allowable operating expenses. Enter the **smaller** of line 15 or line 25				26
27	Limit on excess casualty losses and depreciation. Subtract line 26 from line 15				27
28	Excess casualty losses (see instructions)	28			
29	Depreciation of your home from line 41 below	29			
30	Carryover of excess casualty losses and depreciation from 2007 Form 8829, line 43	30			
31	Add lines 28 through 30				31
32	Allowable excess casualty losses and depreciation. Enter the **smaller** of line 27 or line 31				32
33	Add lines 14, 26, and 32				33
34	Casualty loss portion, if any, from lines 14 and 32. Carry amount to **Form 4684**, Section B				34
35	**Allowable expenses for business use of your home.** Subtract line 34 from line 33. Enter here and on Schedule C, line 30. If your home was used for more than one business, see instructions ▶				35

Part III Depreciation of Your Home

36	Enter the **smaller** of your home's adjusted basis or its fair market value (see instructions)	36	
37	Value of land included on line 36	37	
38	Basis of building. Subtract line 37 from line 36	38	
39	Business basis of building. Multiply line 38 by line 7	39	
40	Depreciation percentage (see instructions)	40	%
41	Depreciation allowable (see instructions). Multiply line 39 by line 40. Enter here and on line 29 above	41	

Part IV Carryover of Unallowed Expenses to 2009

42	Operating expenses. Subtract line 26 from line 25. If less than zero, enter -0-	42	
43	Excess casualty losses and depreciation. Subtract line 32 from line 31. If less than zero, enter -0-	43	

For Paperwork Reduction Act Notice, see page 4 of separate instructions.   Cat. No. 13232M   Form **8829** (2008)

Join The Live Out Loud Community!
Your Entrepreneur Center for
Everything You Need.

FREE and Personal Membership Accounts!

Gain instant access to a wealth of information designed to help you launch into success! Blogs, forums, webinars, podcasts, document downloads, discount "members only" insurance quotes and much more -- all yours with your membership. Build your network of friends to help you along your road to riches and benefit from peer to peer knowledge sharing!

 *Start Now!*

Go to LiveOutLoudCommunity.com
And Join Us Today! Or Call 888-262-2402